Obscenity and Pornography Decisions of the United States Supreme Court

Maureen Harrison & Steve Gilbert
Editors

Excellent Books
Carlsbad, California

EXCELLENT BOOKS
Post Office Box 131322
Carlsbad, CA 92013-1322

Publisher's Cataloging in Publication Data

Obscenity and Pornography Decisions of the United States Supreme Court/
  Maureen Harrison, Steve Gilbert, editors.
    p. cm. -
Bibliography: p.
Includes Index.

1. United States. Supreme Court.
2. Obscenity - Law - United States - Cases.
I. Title. II. Harrison, Maureen. III. Gilbert, Steve.

KF9444.A7O14 2000   LC 00-90223
323.445 O14 2000

ISBN 1-880780-23-2

Introduction

Obscenity (n.) - Offensive to the accepted standards of decency. *Syn.* Immoral, vulgar, crude, lewd, indecent.

Pornography (n.) - Depictions of erotic acts intended to cause sexual excitement. *Syn.* Smutty, filthy, dirty.

What constitutes obscenity? When is a work pornographic? In 1712 the Massachusetts Bay Colony enacted America's first obscenity and pornography law, making it a crime to publish anything judged by their courts to be *Filthy*. Prior to 1933 American courts, by applying Victorian England's *Isolated Passages Test*, found works to be obscene if they contained "any isolated passage that tended to deprave or corrupt upon those whose susceptible minds were open to immoral influences." In 1933 a Federal District Court, applying the *Impure Thoughts Test*, found works to be obscene if they "tended to stir the sex impulses or lead to sexually impure and lustful thoughts." In 1957 the Supreme Court, by applying the *Roth Test*, found works to be obscene if "to the average person, applying contemporary community standards, the dominant theme of the material, taken as a whole, appeals to prurient interest." In 1966 the Supreme Court, applying the *Fanny Hill Test*, found works to be obscene if "they appealed to prurient interest in sex, were patently offensive to community standards relating to sex, and were utterly without redeeming social value." Finally, in 1973 the Supreme Court, by applying the *Miller Test*, found works to be obscene if "the average person, applying contemporary community standards, would find that the work, taken as a whole, appeals to the prurient interest; and whether the work depicts or describes, in a patently offensive way, sexual conduct specifically defined by the applicable state law; and whether the work, taken as a whole, lacks serious literary, artistic, political, or scientific value."

In 1964 Justice Potter Stewart established his own common sense obscenity and pornography test - *I know it when I see it.*

Since its creation in 1791, the Supreme Court has exercised its judicial power to settle all Constitutional controversies arising in the Federal Courts and all Constitutional questions arising in the State Courts. The suppression by federal and state agents of what they believe to be obscenity and pornography versus the First Amendment's Free Speech and Free Press protections is one of those Constitutional controversies.

Justice Benjamin Cardozo wrote this about some of the people whose personal legal problems have reached the United States Supreme Court - *The sordid controversies of litigants are the stuff out of which great and shining truths will ultimately be shaped.* The "sordid controversies" of people involved either in the creation or suppression of works thought to be obscene or pornographic have many times found their way before the Supreme Court to become the "stuff out of which great and shining truths are shaped." These "great and shining truths," the Supreme Court's decisions on what constitutes legal obscenity and pornography, have become binding legal precedents - the settled law of the land.

In its long history, the Supreme Court has issued thousands of individual decisions on constitutional controversies. All have been important to the parties involved, but some - a significant few - are so important as to involve either the constitutional rights or the constitutional restrictions placed upon the rights of all Americans. These are Landmark Decisions, fundamentally altering the relationships of Americans to their institutions and to each other. This book deals with those landmark decisions on obscenity and pornography. Of these significant few, we have selected fourteen decisions on obscenity and pornography for inclusion in this book. Because of its impact on obscenity and pornography law, we include as an Appendix the U.S. District Court's decision in the case of James Joyce's *Ulysses*.

On the first Monday of each October the United States Supreme Court begins a new Term. From all over the country, on all kinds of issues, and for all kinds of reasons, Americans bring controversies to the Court for a final disposition. Every year over five thousand requests for review of lower court decisions are received by the Court. Requests, called *petitions for certiorari*, come to the Court from the losing side in Federal Appeals Courts or State Supreme Courts. Four of the nine Justices must agree to a review. Review is accepted in only about four hundred cases each year. Once accepted, written arguments - briefs, pro and con - are submitted to the Court by both the petitioner (the losing side appealing the lower court's decision against them) and the respondent (the winning side defending the lower court's decision for them). Interested parties, called *amici curiae* (friends of the Court), may be permitted to submit briefs in support of either side. After all submitted briefs are reviewed by the Justices, public oral arguments are heard by the Court. Ordinarily the opposing sides, the petitioner and the respondent, are given thirty minutes of oral argument. The Justices, at their discretion, may interrupt at any time to require further explanations, to pose hypothetical questions, or to make observations. Twice a week, on Wednesdays and Fridays, the Justices meet alone in conference to discuss each case and vote on its outcome. They may affirm [let stand] or reverse [change the outcome of] in whole or in part, the decisions of the lower courts from which these appeals have come. One Justice, voting in the majority, will be selected to write the majority opinion. Others may join in the majority opinion, write their own concurring opinion, write their own dissenting opinion, or join in another's concurrence or dissent. Drafts of the majority, concurring, and dissenting opinions circulate among the Justices, and are redrafted and recirculated until a consensus is reached and a decision is announced. It is the majority opinion as finally issued by the Supreme Court that stands as the law of the land. All other Courts, Federal and State, are bound by Supreme Court precedent. The official legal texts of these decisions are published in the five hundred-plus volumes of *U.S. Reports*.

Judge Learned Hand wrote, *The language of the law must not be foreign to the ears of those who are to obey it.* The Landmark Decisions presented in this book are carefully edited, plain-English versions of the official legal texts issued by the Supreme Court in *United States Reports.* We, as editors, have made every effort to replace esoteric legalese with understandable everyday English without damaging the original decisions. Edited out are long alpha-numeric legal citations and wordy wrangles over points of procedure. Edited in are definitions (*writ of habeas corpus* = an order from a judge to bring a person to court), translations (*certiorari* = the decision of the Court to review a case), identifications (petitioner = the individual appealing a lower court's decision; respondent = the individual defending the lower court's decision), and explanations (where the case originated, how it got to the court, and who all the parties involved were).

You will find in *Obscenity and Pornography Decisions* the majority opinion of the Court as expressed by the Justice chosen to speak for the Court. Preceding each edited decision, we note where the complete decision can be found. The bibliography provides a list of further reading on the issues before the Court.

Chief Justice John Marshall wrote that a Supreme Court decision "comes home in its effect to every man's fireside; it passes on his property, his reputation, his life, his all." We entered into editing books on landmark Supreme Court decisions because we, like you, and your family and friends, must obey, under penalty of law, these decisions. It stands to reason that, if we owe our obedience to what the Supreme Court decides, then we owe it to ourselves to know what they have written, not second-hand, but for ourselves. We believe that every American should *know it when they see it.*

M.H.& S.G.

Table of Contents

"Dial-A-Porn"
Sable Communications v. FCC
73

We have repeatedly held that the protection of the First Amendment does not extend to obscene speech. The cases before us today do not require us to decide what is obscene or what is indecent but rather to determine whether Congress is empowered to prohibit transmission of obscene telephonic communications. (1989)

"Filthy" School Library Books
Island Trees Schools v. Pico
87

[The School Board] characterized the removed books as "anti-American, anti-Christian, anti-Semitic, and just plain filthy," and concluded that "[i]t is our duty, our moral obligation, to protect the children in our schools from this moral danger as surely as from physical and medical dangers." (1982)

Child Pornography
101
New York v. Ferber

[A] work which, taken on the whole, contains serious literary, artistic, political, or scientific value may nevertheless embody the hardest core of child pornography. "It is irrelevant to the child [who has been abused] whether or not the material . . . has a literary, artistic, political or social value." (1982)

The Seven Words You Can't Say On The Radio
FCC v. Pacifica Foundation
117

To say that one may avoid further offense by turning off the radio when he hears indecent language is like saying that the remedy for an assault is to run away after the first blow. (1978)

Sexually Explicit Mail
Miller v. California
137

It is neither realistic nor constitutionally sound to read the First Amendment as requiring that the people of Maine or Mississippi accept public depiction of conduct found tolerable in Las Vegas or New York City. People in different States vary in their tastes and attitudes, and this diversity is not to be strangled by the absolutism of imposed uniformity. (1973)

Pornography And Privacy
Stanley v. Georgia
149

If the First Amendment means anything, it means that a State has no business telling a man, sitting alone in his own house, what books he may read or what films he may watch. Our whole constitutional heritage rebels at the thought of giving government the power to control men's minds. (1969)

Smut Peddling
Ginsberg v. New York
157

"It is . . . altogether fitting and proper for a state to include in a statute designed to regulate the sale of pornography to children special standards, broader than those embodied in legislation aimed at controlling dissemination of such material to adults." (1968)

The Book Banned In Boston
Fanny Hill v. Massachusetts
167

Evidence that [Fanny Hill] was . . . exploited for the sake of prurient appeal, to the exclusion of all other values, might justify the conclusion that the book was utterly without redeeming social importance. (1966)

Publicly Funded "Pornographic" Art
National Endowment for the Arts v. Finley

On September 29, 1965 Congress passed the National Endowment for the Arts and Humanities Act. The National Endowment for the Arts (NEA) was created to award federal funds to American artists and art institutions possessing *Artistic and cultural significance.*

Over 100,000 awards, totaling over $3 billion, were granted without restrictions until 1989, when the NEA angered a majority of Congress by approving public funding for sexually provocative art exhibits, including the highly controversial works of photographer Robert Mapplethorpe. Mapplethorpe's collection of homoerotic photographs was shown, with a $30,000 federal grant, at the University of Pennsylvania's Institute of Contemporary Art.

Outraged by the NEA's use of pubic funds to showcase the works of Mapplethorpe and others, Congress, on November 5, 1990, passed the so-called "Mapplethorpe Amendment," placing "decency" restrictions on the NEA's funding procedures to insure that their would be no future grants to works depicting *Sadomasochism, homoeroticism, the sexual exploitation of children, or individuals engaged in sex acts, and which, when taken as a whole, do not have serious literary, artistic, political, or scientific value.*

A legal challenge to the "Mapplethorpe Amendment" was brought against the NEA by Karen Finley and other performance artists who, under the new "decency" restrictions, had been denied federal funding. On June 9, 1992 the U.S. District Court struck down the "Mapplethorpe Amendment" as unconstitutional. On November 5, 1996 the U.S. Court of Appeals upheld the lower Court. The NEA appealed for a reversal to the United States Supreme Court.

On June 25, 1998 the 7-1 decision of the Court was announced by Associate Justice Sandra Day O'Connor.

The *"Pornographic" Art* Court

Chief Justice William Rehnquist
Appointed Chief Justice by President Reagan
Appointed Associate Justice by President Nixon
Served 1971 -

Associate Justice John Paul Stevens
Appointed by President Ford
Served 1975 -

Associate Justice Sandra Day O'Connor
Appointed by President Reagan
Served 1981 -

Associate Justice Antonin Scalia
Appointed by President Reagan
Served 1986 -

Associate Justice Anthony Kennedy
Appointed by President Reagan
Served 1988 -

Associate Justice David Souter
Appointed by President Bush
Served 1990 -

Associate Justice Clarence Thomas
Appointed by President Bush
Served 1991 -

Associate Justice Ruth Bader Ginsberg
Appointed by President Clinton
Served 1993 -

Associate Justice Stephen Breyer
Appointed by President Clinton
Served 1994 -

The unedited text of *The National Endowment for the Arts v. Finley* can be found in volume 524 of *United States Reports*. Our edited plain-English text follows.

NATIONAL ENDOWMENT
FOR THE ARTS v. FINLEY
June 25, 1998

JUSTICE SANDRA DAY O'CONNOR: The National Foundation on the Arts and Humanities Act, as amended in 1990 [the Mapplethorpe Amendment], requires the Chairperson of the National Endowment for the Arts (NEA) to ensure that "artistic excellence and artistic merit are the criteria by which [grant] applications are judged, taking into consideration general standards of decency and respect for the diverse beliefs and values of the American public." In this case, we review the Court of Appeals' determination that [the Mapplethorpe Amendment], on its face, impermissibly discriminates on the basis of viewpoint and is void for vagueness under the First and Fifth Amendments. We conclude that [the Mapplethorpe Amendment] is . . . valid, as it neither inherently interferes with First Amendment rights nor violates constitutional vagueness principles.

With the establishment of the NEA in 1965, Congress embarked on a "broadly conceived national policy of support for the . . . arts in the United States," pledging federal funds to "help create and sustain not only a climate encouraging freedom of thought, imagination, and inquiry but also the material conditions facilitating the release of . . . creative talent." The enabling statute vests the NEA with substantial discretion to award grants; it identifies only the broadest funding priorities, including "artistic and cultural significance, giving emphasis to American creativity and cultural diversity," "professional excellence," and the encouragement of "public knowledge, education, understanding, and appreciation of the arts."

Applications for NEA funding are initially reviewed by advisory panels composed of experts in the relevant field of the arts. Under the [Mapplethorpe Amendment], those panels must reflect "diverse artistic and cultural points of view" and include "wide geographic, ethnic, and minority representation," as well as "lay individuals who are knowledgeable about the arts." The panels report to the 26-member National Council on the Arts, which, in turn, advises the NEA Chairperson. The Chairperson has the ultimate authority to award grants but may not approve an application as to which the Council has made a negative recommendation.

Since 1965, the NEA has distributed over three billion dollars in grants to individuals and organizations, funding that has served as a catalyst for increased state, corporate, and foundation support for the arts. Congress has recently restricted the availability of federal funding for individual artists, confining grants primarily to qualifying organizations and state arts agencies, and constraining sub-granting. By far the largest portion of the grants distributed in fiscal year 1998 were awarded directly to state arts agencies. In the remaining categories, the most substantial grants were allocated to symphony orchestras, fine arts museums, dance theater foundations, and opera associations.

Throughout the NEA's history, only a handful of the agency's roughly 100,000 awards have generated formal complaints about misapplied funds or abuse of the public's trust. Two provocative works, however, prompted public controversy in 1989 and led to congressional revaluation of the NEA's funding priorities and efforts to increase oversight of its grant-making procedures. The Institute of Contemporary Art at the University of Pennsylvania had used $30,000 of a visual arts grant it received from the NEA to fund a 1989 retrospective of photographer Robert Mapplethorpe's work. The exhibit, entitled *The Perfect Moment*, included homoerotic photographs that several Members of Congress condemned as pornographic. Members also denounced artist Andres Serrano's work *Piss Christ*, a photograph of a crucifix immersed in urine. Serrano had been awarded a $15,000 grant from the Southeast Center for Contemporary Art, an organization that received NEA support.

When considering the NEA's appropriations for fiscal year 1990, Congress reacted to the controversy surrounding the Mapplethorpe and Serrano photographs by eliminating $45,000 from the agency's budget, the precise amount contributed to the two exhibits by NEA grant recipients. Congress also enacted an amendment providing that no NEA funds "may be used to promote, disseminate, or produce materials which in the judgment of [the NEA] may be considered obscene, including but not limited to, depictions of sadomasochism, homoeroticism, the sexual exploitation of children, or individuals engaged in sex acts and which, when taken as a whole, do not have serious literary, artistic, political, or scientific value." The NEA implemented Congress' mandate by instituting a requirement that all grantees certify in writing that they would not utilize federal funding to engage in projects inconsistent with the criteria in the 1990 appropriations bill. That certification requirement was subsequently invalidated as unconstitutionally vague by a Federal District Court, and the NEA did not appeal the decision.

In the 1990 appropriations bill, Congress also agreed to create an Independent Commission of constitutional law scholars to review the NEA's grant-making procedures and assess the possibility of more focused standards for public arts funding. The Commission's report, issued in September 1990, concluded that there is no constitutional obligation to provide arts funding, but also recommended that the NEA rescind the certification requirement and cautioned against legislation setting forth any content restrictions. Instead, the Commission suggested procedural changes to enhance the role of advisory panels and a statutory reaffirmation of "the high place the nation accords to the fostering of mutual respect for the disparate beliefs and values among us."

Informed by the Commission's recommendations, and cognizant of pending judicial challenges to the funding limitations in the 1990 appropriations bill, Congress debated several proposals to reform the NEA's grant-making process when it considered the agency's reauthorization in the fall of 1990. The House rejected the Crane Amendment, which would have virtually eliminated the NEA, and the Rohrabacher Amendment, which would have introduced a prohibition on awarding any grants that could be used to "promote, distribute, disseminate, or produce matter that has the purpose or effect of denigrating the beliefs, tenets, or objects of a particular religion" or "of denigrating an individual, or group of individuals, on the basis of race, sex, handicap, or national origin." Ultimately, Congress adopted the Williams/Coleman Amendment, a bipartisan compromise between Members opposing any funding restrictions and those favoring some guidance to the agency. In relevant part, the Amendment . . . directs the Chairperson in establishing procedures to judge the artistic merit of grant applications, to "tak[e] into consideration general standards of decency and respect for the diverse beliefs and values of the American public."

The NEA has not promulgated any official interpretation of the provision, but in December 1990, the Council unanimously adopted a resolution to implement [the Amendment] merely by ensuring that the members of the advisory panels that conduct the initial review of grant applications represent geographic, ethnic, and aesthetic diversity. John Frohnmayer, then Chairperson of the NEA, also declared that he would "count on [the] procedures" ensuring diverse membership on the peer review panels to fulfill Congress' mandate.

The four individual respondents in this case, Karen Finley, John Fleck, Holly Hughes, and Tim Miller, are performance artists who applied for NEA grants before [the Amendment] was enacted. An advisory panel recommended approval of [their] projects, both initially and after receiving Frohnmayer's request to reconsider three of the applications. A majority of the Council subsequently recommended disapproval, and in June 1990, the NEA informed [them] that they had been denied funding. [The four] filed suit, alleging that the NEA had violated their First Amendment rights by rejecting the applications on political grounds, had failed to follow statutory procedures by basing the denial on criteria other than those set forth in the NEA's enabling statute, and had breached the confidentiality of their grant applications through the release of quotations to the press, in violation of the Privacy Act of 1974. [The four] sought restoration of the recommended grants or reconsideration of their applications, as well as damages for the alleged Privacy Act violations. When Congress enacted [the Amendment, the four], now joined by the National Association of Artists' Organizations (NAAO), amended their complaint to challenge the provision as void for vagueness and impermissibly viewpoint-based.

. . . [T]he NEA agreed to settle the . . . claims by paying the artists the amount of the vetoed grants, damages, and attorney's fees.

The District Court then [found in favor of the four] on their . . . constitutional challenge to [the Amendment] and enjoined [prohibited] enforcement of the provision. The court rejected the argument that the NEA could comply with [the Amendment] by structuring the grant selection process to provide for diverse advisory panels. The provision, the court stated, "fails adequately to notify applicants of what is required of them or to circumscribe NEA discretion." Reasoning that "the very nature of our pluralistic society is that there are an infinite number of values and beliefs, and correlatively, there may be no national 'general standards of decency,'" the court concluded that [the Amendment] "cannot be given effect consistent with the Fifth Amendment's due process requirement." . . . The Government did not seek a stay [halting] of the District Court's injunction [a court order stopping an action], and consequently the NEA has not applied [the Amendment] since June 1992.

A divided panel of the Court of Appeals affirmed [upheld] the District Court's ruling. . . . [The Court of Appeals] ruled that [the Amendment] violates the First Amendment's prohibition on viewpoint-based restrictions on protected speech. Government funding of the arts, the court explained, is both a "traditional sphere of free expression," and an area in which the Government has stated its intention to "encourage a diversity of views from private speakers." Accordingly, finding that [the Amendment] "has a speech-based restriction as its sole rationale and operative principle," and noting the NEA's failure to articulate a compelling interest for the provision, the court declared it . . . invalid.

The dissent asserted that the First Amendment protects artists' rights to express themselves as indecently and disrespectfully as they like, but does not compel the Government to fund that speech. The challenged provision, the dissent contended, did not prohibit the NEA from funding indecent or offensive art, but merely required the agency to consider the "decency and respect" criteria in the grant selection process. Moreover, according to the dissent's reasoning, the vagueness principles applicable to the direct regulation of speech have no bearing on the selective award of prizes, and the Government may draw distinctions based on content and viewpoint in making its funding decisions. . . .

We granted certiorari [agreed to hear the case], and now reverse the judgment of the Court of Appeals.

[The four] raise a . . . constitutional challenge to [the Amendment], and consequently they confront "a heavy burden" in advancing their claim. . . . To prevail, [they] must demonstrate a substantial risk that application of the provision will lead to the suppression of speech.

[They] argue that the provision is a paradigmatic example of viewpoint discrimination because it rejects any artistic speech that either fails to respect mainstream values or offends standards of decency. The premise of [their] claim is that [the Amendment] constrains the agency's ability to fund certain categories of artistic expression. The NEA, however, . . . contends that it stops well short of an absolute restriction. [The Amendment] adds "considerations" to the grant-making process; it does not preclude awards to projects that might be deemed "indecent" or "disrespectful," nor place conditions on grants, or even specify that those factors must be given any particular weight in reviewing an application. Indeed, the agency asserts that it has adequately implemented [the Amendment] merely by ensuring the representation of various backgrounds and points of view on the advisory panels that analyze grant applications. We do not decide whether the NEA's view - that the formulation of diverse advisory panels is sufficient to comply with Congress' command - is in fact a reasonable reading of the statute. It is clear, however, that the text of [the Amendment] imposes no categorical requirement. The advisory language stands in sharp contrast to congressional efforts to prohibit the funding of certain classes of speech. When Congress has in fact intended to affirmatively constrain the NEA's grant-making authority, it has done so in no uncertain terms.

Furthermore, like the plain language of [the Mapplethorpe Amendment], the political context surrounding the adoption of the "decency and respect" clause is inconsistent with [the four's] assertion that the provision compels the NEA to deny funding on the basis of viewpoint discriminatory criteria. The legislation was a bipartisan proposal introduced as a counterweight to amendments aimed at eliminating the NEA's funding or substantially constraining its grant-making authority. The Independent Commission had cautioned Congress against the adoption of distinct viewpoint-based standards for funding, and the Commission's report suggests that "additional criteria for selection, if any, should be incorporated as part of the selection process (perhaps as part of a definition of 'artistic excellence'), rather than isolated and treated as exogenous considerations." In keeping with that recommendation, the criteria in [the Amendment] inform the assessment of artistic merit, but Congress declined to disallow any particular viewpoints. As the sponsors of [the Amendment] noted in urging rejection of the Rohrabacher Amendment, "if we start down that road of prohibiting categories of expression, categories which are indeed constitutionally protected speech, where do we end? Where one Member's aversions end, others with different sensibilities and with different values begin." In contrast, before the vote on [the Amendment], one of its sponsors stated, "If we have done one important thing in this amendment, it is this. We have maintained the integrity of freedom of expression in the United States."

That [the Amendment] admonishes the NEA merely to take "decency and respect" into consideration, and that the legislation was aimed at reforming procedures rather than precluding speech, undercut [the four's] argument that the provision inevitably will be utilized as a tool for invidious viewpoint discrimination. In cases where we have struck down legislation as . . . unconstitutional, the dangers were both more evident and more substantial. In *R.A.V. v. St. Paul*, for example, we invalidated . . . a municipal ordinance that defined as a criminal offense the placement of a symbol on public or private property "'which one knows or has reasonable grounds to know arouses anger, alarm, or resentment in others on the basis of race, color, creed, religion, or gender.'" That provision set forth a clear penalty, proscribed views on particular "disfavored subjects," and suppressed "distinctive idea[s], conveyed by a distinctive message."

In contrast, the "decency and respect" criteria do not silence speakers by expressly "threaten[ing] censorship of ideas." Thus, we do not perceive a realistic danger that [the Amendment] will compromise First Amendment values. As [the four's] own arguments demonstrate, the considerations that the provision introduces, by their nature, do not engender the kind of directed viewpoint discrimination that would prompt this Court to invalidate a statute. . . . [The four] assert, for example, that "[o]ne would be hard-pressed to find two people in the United States who could agree on what the 'diverse beliefs and values of the American public' are, much less on whether a particular work of art 'respects' them"; and they claim that "'[d]ecency' is likely to mean something very different to a septegenarian in Tuscaloosa and a teenager in Las Vegas." The NEA likewise views the considerations enumerated in [the Amendment] as susceptible to multiple interpretations. Accordingly, the provision does not introduce considerations that, in practice, would effectively preclude or punish the expression of particular views. Indeed, one could hardly anticipate how "decency" or "respect" would bear on grant applications in categories such as funding for symphony orchestras.

[The four's] claim that the provision is . . . unconstitutional may be reduced to the argument that the criteria in [the Amendment] are sufficiently subjective that the agency could utilize them to engage in viewpoint discrimination. Given the varied interpretations of the criteria and the vague exhortation to "take them into consideration," it seems unlikely that this provision will introduce any greater element of selectivity than the determination of "artistic excellence" itself. And we are reluctant, in any event, to invalidate legislation "on the basis of its hypothetical application to situations not before the Court."

The [Act establishing the NEA] contemplates a number of indisputably constitutional applications for both the "decency" prong of [the Mapplethorpe Amendment] and its reference to "respect for the diverse beliefs and values of the American public." Educational programs are central to the NEA's mission. And it is well established that "decency" is a permissible factor where "educational suitability" motivates its consideration.

Permissible applications of the mandate to consider "respect for the diverse beliefs and values of the American public" are also apparent. In setting forth the purposes of the NEA, Congress explained that "[i]t is vital to democracy to honor and preserve its multicultural artistic heritage." The agency expressly takes diversity into account, giving special consideration to "projects and productions . . . that reach, or reflect the culture of, a minority, inner city, rural, or tribal community," as well as projects that generally emphasize "cultural diversity." [The four] do not contend that the criteria in [the Amendment] are impermissibly applied when they may be justified, as the statute contemplates, with respect to a project's intended audience.

We recognize, of course, that reference to these permissible applications would not alone be sufficient to sustain [uphold] the statute against [this] First Amendment challenge. But neither are we persuaded that, in other applications, the language of [the Amendment] itself will give rise to the suppression of protected expression. Any content-based considerations that may be taken into account in the grant-making process are a consequence of the nature of arts funding. The NEA has limited resources and it must deny the majority of the grant applications that it receives, including many that propose "artistically excellent" projects. The agency may decide to fund particular projects for a wide variety of reasons, "such as the technical proficiency of the artist, the creativity of the work, the anticipated public interest in or appreciation of the work, the work's contemporary relevance, its educational value, its suitability for or appeal to special audiences (such as children or the disabled), its service to a rural or isolated community, or even simply that the work could increase public knowledge of an art form." As [Judge Andrew Kleinfeld of the Court of Appeals] noted [in his dissent], it would be "impossible to have a highly selective grant program without denying money to a large amount of constitutionally ·protected expression." The "very assumption" of the NEA is that grants will be awarded according to the "artistic worth of competing applications," and absolute neutrality is simply "inconceivable." . . .

[The four] do not allege discrimination in any particular funding decision. (In fact, after filing suit to challenge [the Amendment], two of the individual respondents [Hughes and Miller] received NEA grants. Thus, we have no occasion here to address an as-applied challenge in a situation where the denial of a grant may be shown to be the product of invidious viewpoint discrimination. If the NEA were to leverage its power to award subsidies on the basis of subjective criteria into a penalty on disfavored viewpoints, then we would confront a different case. We have stated that, even in the provision of subsidies, the Government may not "ai[m] at the suppression of dangerous ideas," and if a subsidy were "manipulated" to have a "coercive effect," then relief could be appropriate. In addition, as the NEA itself concedes, a more pressing constitutional question would arise if government funding resulted in the imposition of a disproportionate burden calculated to drive "certain ideas or viewpoints from the marketplace." Unless and until [the Amendment] is applied in a manner that raises concern about the suppression of disfavored viewpoints, however, we uphold the constitutionality of the provision.

Finally, . . . we note that the Government may allocate competitive funding according to criteria that would be impermissible were direct regulation of speech or a criminal penalty at stake. So long as legislation does not infringe on other constitutionally protected rights, Congress has wide latitude to set spending priorities. In the 1990 Amendments . . . , Congress modified the declaration of purpose in the NEA's enabling act to provide that arts funding should "contribute to public support and confidence in the use of taxpayer funds," and that "[p]ublic funds . . . must ultimately serve public purposes the Congress defines." And as we held in *Rust [v. Sullivan]*, Congress may "selectively fund a program to encourage certain activities it believes to be in the public interest, without at the same time funding an alternative program which seeks to deal with the problem in another way." In doing so, "the Government has not discriminated on the basis of viewpoint; it has merely chosen to fund one activity to the exclusion of the other."

The lower courts also erred in invalidating [the Amendment] as unconstitutionally vague. Under the First and Fifth Amendments, speakers are protected from arbitrary and discriminatory enforcement of vague standards. The terms of the provision are undeniably opaque, and if they appeared in a criminal statute or regulatory scheme, they could raise substantial vagueness concerns. It is unlikely, however, that speakers will be compelled to steer too far clear of any "forbidden area" in the context of grants of this nature. We recognize, as a practical matter, that artists may conform their speech to what they believe to be the decision-making criteria in order to acquire funding. But when the Government is acting as patron rather than as sovereign, the consequences of imprecision are not constitutionally severe.

In the context of selective subsidies, it is not always feasible for Congress to legislate with clarity. Indeed, if this statute is unconstitutionally vague, then so too are all government programs awarding scholarships and grants on the basis of subjective criteria such as "excellence." To accept [the] vagueness argument would be to call into question the constitutionality of these valuable government programs and countless others like them.

[The Amendment] merely adds some imprecise considerations to an already subjective selection process. It does not . . . impermissibly infringe on First or Fifth Amendment rights. Accordingly, the judgment of the Court of Appeals is reversed and the case is remanded [returned] for further proceedings consistent with this opinion.

The Indecent Internet
Reno v. American Civil Liberties Union

On February 8, 1996 Congress passed, and the President signed into law, the Communications Decency Act (CDA), which contained two provisions by which minors were to be denied access to any messages or images on the Internet determined to be either "indecent" or "offensive."

The *Indecent Transmissions* provision, aimed at e-mail, newsgroups, and chatrooms, prohibited Internet users from sending to anyone under eighteen years of age *Any comment, request, suggestion, proposal, image, or other communication which is obscene or indecent . . . regardless of whether the user of such service placed the call or initiated the communication.*

The *Offensive Displays* provision, aimed at "adult" websites, prohibited Internet users from sending to anyone under eighteen years of age *Any comment, request, suggestion, proposal, image, or other communication that, in context, depicts or describes, in terms patently offensive as measured by contemporary community standards, sexual or excretory activities or organs, regardless of whether the user of such service placed the call or initiated the communication.*

The American Civil Liberties Union (ACLU), joined by the American Library Association (ALA), and others, brought suit in U.S. District Court against the U.S. Government, in the person of Attorney General Janet Reno. They challenged the constitutionality, under the First Amendment, of these two CDA provisions.

On June 11, 1996 the U.S. District Court, finding that *The Internet is entitled to the highest protection from government intrusion*, found these provisions of the CDA unconstitutional. Attorney General Reno appealed for a reversal to the United States Supreme Court.

On June 26, 1997 the 7-2 decision of the Court was announced by Associate Justice John Paul Stevens.

The *Indecent Internet* Court

Chief Justice William Rehnquist
Appointed Chief Justice by President Reagan
Appointed Associate Justice by President Nixon
Served 1971 -

Associate Justice John Paul Stevens
Appointed by President Ford
Served 1975 -

Associate Justice Sandra Day O'Connor
Appointed by President Reagan
Served 1981 -

Associate Justice Antonin Scalia
Appointed by President Reagan
Served 1986 -

Associate Justice Anthony Kennedy
Appointed by President Reagan
Served 1988 -

Associate Justice David Souter
Appointed by President Bush
Served 1990 -

Associate Justice Clarence Thomas
Appointed by President Bush
Served 1991 -

Associate Justice Ruth Bader Ginsberg
Appointed by President Clinton
Served 1993 -

Associate Justice Stephen Breyer
Appointed by President Clinton
Served 1994 -

The unedited text of *Reno v. ACLU* can be found in volume 521 of *United States Reports*. Our edited plain-English text follows.

RENO v.
AMERICAN CIVIL LIBERTIES UNION
June 26, 1997

JUSTICE JOHN PAUL STEVENS: At issue is the constitutionality of two statutory provisions enacted to protect
minors from "indecent" and "patently offensive" communications on the Internet. Notwithstanding the legitimacy and
importance of the congressional goal of protecting children
from harmful materials, we agree with the three-judge District Court that the statute abridges "the freedom of
speech" protected by the First Amendment.

. . . . The [District Court's] findings describe the character
and the dimensions of the Internet, the availability of sexually explicit material in that medium, and the problems con-
fronting age verification for recipients of Internet communications. Because those findings provide the underpinnings
for the legal issues, we begin with a summary of the undisputed facts.

The Internet is an international network of interconnected
computers. It is the outgrowth of what began in 1969 as a
military program. . . , which was designed to enable computers operated by the military, defense contractors, and
universities conducting defense-related research to communicate with one another by redundant channels even if
some portions of the network were damaged in a war.
While the [program] no longer exists, it provided an example for the development of a number of civilian networks
that, eventually linking with each other, now enable tens of
millions of people to communicate with one another and to
access vast amounts of information from around the world.
The Internet is "a unique and wholly new medium of
worldwide human communication."

The Internet has experienced "extraordinary growth." The number of "host" computers - those that store information and relay communications - increased from about 300 in 1981 to approximately 9,400,000 by the time of the trial in 1996. Roughly 60% of these hosts are located in the United States. About 40 million people used the Internet at the time of trial, a number that is expected to mushroom to 200 million by 1999.

Individuals can obtain access to the Internet from many different sources, generally hosts themselves or entities with a host affiliation. Most colleges and universities provide access for their students and faculty; many corporations provide their employees with access through an office network; many communities and local libraries provide free access; and an increasing number of storefront "computer coffee shops" provide access for a small hourly fee. Several major national "online services" such as America Online, CompuServe, the Microsoft Network, and Prodigy offer access to their own extensive proprietary networks as well as a link to the much larger resources of the Internet. These commercial online services had almost 12 million individual subscribers at the time of trial.

Anyone with access to the Internet may take advantage of a wide variety of communication and information retrieval methods. These methods are constantly evolving and difficult to categorize precisely. But, as presently constituted, those most relevant to this case are electronic mail ("e-mail"), automatic mailing list services ("mail exploders," sometimes referred to as "listservs"), "newsgroups," "chat rooms," and the "World Wide Web." All of these methods can be used to transmit text; most can transmit sound, pictures, and moving video images. Taken together, these tools constitute a unique medium - known to its users as "cyberspace" - located in no particular geographical location but available to anyone, anywhere in the world, with access to the Internet.

E-mail enables an individual to send an electronic message - generally akin to a note or letter - to another individual or to a group of addressees. The message is generally stored electronically, sometimes waiting for the recipient to check her "mailbox" and sometimes making its receipt known through some type of prompt. A mail exploder is a sort of e-mail group. Subscribers can send messages to a common e-mail address, which then forwards the message to the group's other subscribers. Newsgroups also serve groups of regular participants, but these postings may be read by others as well. There are thousands of such groups, each serving to foster an exchange of information or opinion on a particular topic running the gamut from, say, the music of Wagner to Balkan politics to AIDS prevention to the Chicago Bulls. About 100,000 new messages are posted every day. In most newsgroups, postings are automatically purged at regular intervals. In addition to posting a message that can be read later, two or more individuals wishing to communicate more immediately can enter a chat room to engage in real-time dialogue - in other words, by typing messages to one another that appear almost immediately on the others' computer screens. The District Court found that at any given time "tens of thousands of users are engaging in conversations on a huge range of subjects." It is "no exaggeration to conclude that the content on the Internet is as diverse as human thought."

The best known category of communication over the Internet is the World Wide Web, which allows users to search for and retrieve information stored in remote computers, as well as, in some cases, to communicate back to designated sites. In concrete terms, the Web consists of a vast number of documents stored in different computers all over the world. Some of these documents are simply files containing information. However, more elaborate documents, commonly known as Web "pages," are also prevalent. Each has its own address - "rather like a telephone number." Web pages frequently contain information and sometimes allow the viewer to communicate with the page's (or "site's") author. They generally also contain "links" to other documents created by that site's author or to other (generally) related sites. Typically, the links are either blue or underlined text - sometimes images.

Navigating the Web is relatively straightforward. A user may either type the address of a known page or enter one or more keywords into a commercial "search engine" in an effort to locate sites on a subject of interest. A particular Web page may contain the information sought by the "surfer," or, through its links, it may be an avenue to other documents located anywhere on the Internet. Users generally explore a given Web page, or move to another, by clicking a computer "mouse" on one of the page's icons or links. Access to most Web pages is freely available, but some allow access only to those who have purchased the right from a commercial provider. The Web is thus comparable, from the readers' viewpoint, to both a vast library including millions of readily available and indexed publications and a sprawling mall offering goods and services.

From the publishers' point of view, it constitutes a vast platform from which to address and hear from a world-wide audience of millions of readers, viewers, researchers, and buyers. Any person or organization with a computer connected to the Internet can "publish" information. Publishers include government agencies, educational institutions, commercial entities, advocacy groups, and individuals. Publishers may either make their material available to the entire pool of Internet users, or confine access to a selected group, such as those willing to pay for the privilege. "No single organization controls any membership in the Web, nor is there any centralized point from which individual Web sites or services can be blocked from the Web."

Sexually explicit material on the Internet includes text, pictures, and chat and "extends from the modestly titillating to the hardest-core." These files are created, named, and posted in the same manner as material that is not sexually explicit, and may be accessed either deliberately or unintentionally during the course of an imprecise search. "Once a provider posts its content on the Internet, it cannot prevent that content from entering any community." Thus, for example,

> "when the UCR/California Museum of Photography posts to its Web site nudes by Edward Weston and Robert Mapplethorpe to announce that its new exhibit will travel to Baltimore and New York City, those images are available not only in Los Angeles, Baltimore, and New York City, but also in Cincinnati, Mobile, or Beijing - wherever Internet users live. Similarly, the safer sex instructions that Critical Path posts to its Web site, written in street language so that the teenage receiver can understand them, are available not just in Philadelphia, but also in Provo and Prague."

Some of the communications over the Internet that originate in foreign countries are also sexually explicit.

Though such material is widely available, users seldom encounter such content accidentally. "A document's title or a description of the document will usually appear before the document itself . . . and in many cases the user will receive detailed information about a site's content before he or she need take the step to access the document. Almost all sexually explicit images are preceded by warnings as to the content." For that reason, the "odds are slim" that a user would enter a sexually explicit site by accident. Unlike communi-

cations received by radio or television, "the receipt of information on the Internet requires a series of affirmative
steps more deliberate and directed than merely turning a
dial. A child requires some sophistication and some ability
to read to retrieve material and thereby to use the Internet
unattended."

Systems have been developed to help parents control the
material that may be available on a home computer with
Internet access. A system may either limit a computer's access to an approved list of sources that have been identified
as containing no adult material, it may block designated inappropriate sites, or it may attempt to block messages containing identifiable objectionable features. "Although parental control software currently can screen for certain suggestive words or for known sexually explicit sites, it cannot
now screen for sexually explicit images." Nevertheless, the
evidence indicates that "a reasonably effective method by
which parents can prevent their children from accessing
sexually explicit and other material which parents may believe is inappropriate for their children will soon be available."

The problem of age verification differs for different uses of
the Internet. The District Court categorically determined
that there "is no effective way to determine the identity or
the age of a user who is accessing material through e-mail,
mail exploders, newsgroups, or chat rooms." The Government offered no evidence that there was a reliable way to
screen recipients and participants [on the Internet] for age.
Moreover, even if it were technologically feasible to block
minors' access to newsgroups and chat rooms containing
discussions of art, politics, or other subjects that potentially
elicit "indecent" or "patently offensive" contributions, it
would not be possible to block their access to that material
and "still allow them access to the remaining content, even

if the overwhelming majority of that content was not indecent."

Technology exists by which an operator of a Web site may condition access on the verification of requested information such as a credit card number or an adult password. . . .

[T]he District Court found,

"Even if credit card verification or adult password verification were implemented, the Government presented no testimony as to how such systems could ensure that the user of the password or credit card is in fact over 18. The burdens imposed by credit card verification and adult password verification systems make them effectively unavailable to a substantial number of Internet content providers."

The Telecommunications Act of 1996 was an unusually important legislative enactment. As stated on the first of its 103 pages, its primary purpose was to reduce regulation and encourage "the rapid deployment of new telecommunications technologies." The major components of the statute have nothing to do with the Internet; they were designed to promote competition in the local telephone service market, the multichannel video market, and the market for over-the-air broadcasting. The Act includes seven Titles, six of which are the product of extensive committee hearings and the subject of discussion in Reports prepared by Committees of the Senate and the House of Representatives. By contrast, Title V - known as the "Communications Decency Act of 1996" (CDA) - contains provisions that were either added in executive committee after the hearings were concluded or as amendments offered during floor debate on the legislation. An amendment offered in the Senate was the source of the two statutory provisions challenged in this case. They are informally described as the "indecent transmission" provi-

sion and the "patently offensive display" provision. The first
. . . prohibits the knowing transmission of obscene or indecent messages to any recipient under 18 years of age. It
provides in pertinent part:

> "(a) Whoever -
>> "(1) in interstate or foreign communications - . . . . .
>>> "(B) by means of a telecommunications device
knowingly -
>>>> "(i) makes, creates, or solicits, and
>>>> "(ii) initiates the transmission of,
>>>>> "any comment, request, suggestion, pro-
posal, image, or other communication which
is obscene or indecent, knowing that the recipient of the communication is under 18
years of age, regardless of whether the
maker of such communication placed the
call or initiated the communication; . . . .
>> "(2) knowingly permits any telecommunications facil-
ity under his control to be used for any activity prohibited by paragraph (1) with the intent that it be used
for such activity,
> "shall be fined under Title 18, or imprisoned not more
than two years, or both."

The second provision . . . prohibits the knowing sending or
displaying of patently offensive messages in a manner that
is available to a person under 18 years of age. It provides:

> "(d) Whoever -
>> "(1) in interstate or foreign communications know-
ingly -
>>> "(A) uses an interactive computer service to send
to a specific person or persons under 18 years of
age, or

"(B) uses any interactive computer service to display in a manner available to a person under 18 years of age,

"any comment, request, suggestion, proposal, image, or other communication that, in context, depicts or describes, in terms patently offensive as measured by contemporary community standards, sexual or excretory activities or organs, regardless of whether the user of such service placed the call or initiated the communication; or

"(2) knowingly permits any telecommunications facility under such person's control to be used for an activity prohibited by paragraph (1) with the intent that it be used for such activity,

"shall be fined under Title 18, or imprisoned not more than two years, or both."

The breadth of these prohibitions is qualified by two affirmative defenses. One covers those who take "good faith, reasonable, effective, and appropriate actions" to restrict access by minors to the prohibited communications. The other covers those who restrict access to covered material by requiring certain designated forms of age proof, such as a verified credit card or an adult identification number or code.

On February 8, 1996, immediately after the President signed the statute, 20 plaintiffs filed suit against the Attorney General of the United States and the Department of Justice challenging the constitutionality of [the two provisions, the indecent transmissions provision and the offensive displays provision]. . . . [T]he two cases were consolidated, and a three-judge District Court . . . [unanimously] . . . entered a preliminary injunction [a court order stopping an action] against enforcement of both of the challenged provisions. . . .

The Government appealed under the Act's special review provisions, and we [agreed to hear the case]. In its appeal, the Government argues that the District Court erred in holding that the CDA violated both the First Amendment because it is overbroad and the Fifth Amendment because it is vague. . . . [W]e conclude that the judgment should be affirmed [upheld] without [addressing] the Fifth Amendment issue. . . .

In arguing for reversal, the Government contends that the CDA is plainly constitutional under three of our prior decisions: (1) *Ginsberg v. New York*; (2) *FCC v. Pacifica Foundation*; and (3) *Renton v. Playtime Theatres, Inc.* A close look at these cases, however, raises - rather than relieves - doubts concerning the constitutionality of the CDA.

In *Ginsberg*, we upheld the constitutionality of a New York statute that prohibited selling to minors under 17 years of age material that was considered obscene as to them even if not obscene as to adults. We rejected the defendant's broad submission that "the scope of the constitutional freedom of expression secured to a citizen to read or see material concerned with sex cannot be made to depend on whether the citizen is an adult or a minor." In rejecting that contention, we relied not only on the State's independent interest in the well-being of its youth, but also on our consistent recognition of the principle that "the parents' claim to authority in their own household to direct the rearing of their children is basic in the structure of our society."

In four important respects, the statute upheld in *Ginsberg* was narrower than the CDA. First, we noted in *Ginsberg* that "the prohibition against sales to minors does not bar parents who so desire from purchasing the magazines for their children." Under the CDA, by contrast, neither the parents' consent - nor even their participation - in the communication would avoid the application of the statute.

Second, the New York statute applied only to commercial transactions, whereas the CDA contains no such limitation. Third, the New York statute cabined its definition of material that is harmful to minors with the requirement that it be "utterly without redeeming social importance for minors." The CDA fails to provide us with any definition of the term "indecent" . . . and, importantly, omits any requirement that the "patently offensive" material . . . lack serious literary, artistic, political, or scientific value. Fourth, the New York statute defined a minor as a person under the age of 17, whereas the CDA, in applying to all those under 18 years, includes an additional year of those nearest majority.

In *Pacifica*, we upheld [an] order of the Federal Communications Commission, holding that the broadcast of a recording of a 12-minute monologue entitled "Filthy Words" that had previously been delivered to a live audience "could have been the subject of administrative sanctions." The Commission had found that the repetitive use of certain words referring to excretory or sexual activities or organs "in an afternoon broadcast when children are in the audience was patently offensive" and concluded that the monologue was indecent "as broadcast." . . . [W]e confronted its two constitutional arguments: (1) that the Commission's construction of its authority to ban indecent speech was so broad that its order had to be set aside even if the broadcast at issue was unprotected; and (2) that since the recording was not obscene, the First Amendment forbade any abridgement of the right to broadcast it on the radio. . . . [T]he availability of constitutional protection for a vulgar and offensive monologue that was not obscene depended on the context of the broadcast. Relying on the premise that "of all forms of communication" broadcasting had received the most limited First Amendment protection, the Court concluded that the ease with which children may obtain access to broadcasts, "coupled with the concerns recognized in *Ginsberg*," justified special treatment of indecent broadcasting.

As with the New York statute at issue in *Ginsberg*, there are significant differences between the order upheld in *Pacifica* and the CDA. First, the order in *Pacifica*, issued by an agency that had been regulating radio stations for decades, targeted a specific broadcast that represented a rather dramatic departure from traditional program content in order to designate when - rather than whether - it would be permissible to air such a program in that particular medium. The CDA's broad categorical prohibitions are not limited to particular times and are not dependent on any evaluation by an agency familiar with the unique characteristics of the Internet. Second, unlike the CDA, the Commission's . . . order was not punitive; we expressly refused to decide whether the indecent broadcast "would justify a criminal prosecution." Finally, the Commission's order applied to a medium which as a matter of history had "received the most limited First Amendment protection," in large part because warnings could not adequately protect the listener from unexpected program content. The Internet, however, has no comparable history. Moreover, the District Court found that the risk of encountering indecent material by accident is remote because a series of affirmative steps is required to access specific material.

In *Renton*, we upheld a zoning ordinance that kept adult movie theatres out of residential neighborhoods. The ordinance was aimed, not at the content of the films shown in the theaters, but rather at the "secondary effects" - such as crime and deteriorating property values - that these theaters fostered - "'It is th[e] secondary effect which these zoning ordinances attempt to avoid, not the dissemination of "offensive" speech.'" According to the Government, the CDA is constitutional because it constitutes a sort of "cyberzoning" on the Internet. But the CDA applies broadly to the entire universe of cyberspace. And the purpose of the CDA is to protect children from the primary effects of "indecent" and "patently offensive" speech, rather than any "secondary" effect of such speech. Thus, the CDA is a content-based blanket restriction on speech, and, as such, cannot be "properly analyzed as a form of time, place, and manner regulation."

These precedents, then, surely do not require us to uphold the CDA and are fully consistent with the application of the most stringent review of its provisions.

In *Southeastern Promotions, Ltd. v. Conrad*, we observed that "[e]ach medium of expression . . . may present its own problems." Thus, some of our cases have recognized special justifications for regulation of the broadcast media that are not applicable to other speakers. In these cases, the Court relied on the history of extensive government regulation of the broadcast medium, the scarcity of available frequencies at its inception, and its "invasive" nature.

Those factors are not present in cyberspace. Neither before nor after the enactment of the CDA ha[s] . . . the Internet been subject to the type of government supervision and regulation that has attended the broadcast industry. Moreover, the Internet is not as "invasive" as radio or television. . . .

In *Sable [Communications v. FCC]*, a company engaged in the business of offering sexually-oriented prerecorded telephone messages (popularly known as "dial-a-porn") challenged the constitutionality of an amendment to the Communications Act that imposed a blanket prohibition on indecent as well as obscene interstate commercial telephone messages. . . . "[T]here is a compelling interest in protecting the physical and psychological well-being of minors" which extend[s] to shielding them from indecent messages that are not obscene by adult standards. . . . "[T]he dial-it medium requires the listener to take affirmative steps to receive the communication." "Placing a telephone call," we continued, "is not the same as turning on a radio and being taken by surprise by an indecent message."

Finally, unlike the conditions that prevailed when Congress first authorized regulation of the broadcast spectrum, the Internet can hardly be considered a "scarce" expressive commodity. It provides relatively unlimited, low-cost capacity for communication of all kinds. The Government estimates that "[a]s many as 40 million people use the Internet today, and that figure is expected to grow to 200 million by 1999." This dynamic, multifaceted category of communication includes not only traditional print and news services, but also audio, video, and still images, as well as interactive, real-time dialogue. Through the use of chat rooms, any person with a phone line can become a town crier with a voice that resonates farther than it could from any soapbox. Through the use of Web pages, mail exploders, and newsgroups, the same individual can become a pamphleteer. As the District Court found, "the content on the Internet is as diverse as human thought." We agree with its conclusion that our cases provide no basis for qualifying the level of First Amendment scrutiny that should be applied to this medium.

Regardless of whether the CDA is so vague that it violates the Fifth Amendment, the many ambiguities concerning the scope of its coverage render it problematic for purposes of the First Amendment. For instance, each of the two parts of the CDA uses a different linguistic form. The first uses the word "indecent," while the second speaks of material that "in context, depicts or describes, in terms patently offensive as measured by contemporary community standards, sexual or excretory activities or organs." Given the absence of a definition of either term, this difference in language will provoke uncertainty among speakers about how the two standards relate to each other and just what they mean. Could a speaker confidently assume that a serious discussion about birth control practices, homosexuality, the First Amendment issues raised by the Appendix to our *Pacifica* opinion, or the consequences of prison rape, would not violate the CDA? This uncertainty undermines the likelihood that the CDA has been carefully tailored to the congressional goal of protecting minors from potentially harmful materials.

The vagueness of the CDA is a matter of special concern for two reasons. First, the CDA is a content-based regulation of speech. The vagueness of such a regulation raises special First Amendment concerns because of its obvious chilling effect on free speech. Second, the CDA is a criminal statute. In addition to the opprobrium and stigma of a criminal conviction, the CDA threatens violators with penalties including up to two years in prison for each act of violation. The severity of criminal sanctions may well cause speakers to remain silent rather than communicate even arguably unlawful words, ideas, and images. As a practical matter, this increased deterrent effect, coupled with the "risk of discriminatory enforcement" of vague regulations, poses greater First Amendment concerns than those implicated by the civil regulation reviewed in *Denver Telecommunications v. FCC.*

The Government argues that the statute is no more vague than the obscenity standard this Court established in *Miller v. California.* But that is not so. In *Miller,* this Court reviewed a criminal conviction against a commercial vendor who mailed brochures containing pictures of sexually explicit activities to individuals who had not requested such materials. Having struggled for some time to establish a definition of obscenity, we set forth in *Miller* the test for obscenity that controls to this day:

"(a) whether the average person, applying contemporary community standards, would find that the work, taken as a whole, appeals to the prurient interest; (b) whether the work depicts or describes, in a patently offensive way, sexual conduct specifically defined by the applicable state law; and (c) whether the work, taken as a whole, lacks serious literary, artistic, political, or scientific value."

Because the CDA's "patently offensive" standard (and, we assume arguendo [for the sake of argument], its synonymous "indecent" standard) is one part of the three-prong *Miller* test, the Government reasons, it cannot be unconstitutionally vague.

The Government's assertion is incorrect as a matter of fact. The second prong of the *Miller* test . . . contains a critical requirement that is omitted from the CDA - that the proscribed material be "specifically defined by the applicable state law." This requirement reduces the vagueness inherent in the open-ended term "patently offensive" as used in the CDA. Moreover, the *Miller* definition is limited to "sexual conduct," whereas the CDA extends also to include (1) "excretory activities" as well as (2) "organs" of both a sexual and excretory nature.

The Government's reasoning is also flawed. Just because a definition including three limitations is not vague, it does not follow that one of those limitations, standing by itself, is not vague. Each of *Miller*'s additional two prongs - (1) that, taken as a whole, the material appeal to the "prurient" interest, and (2) that it "lac[k] serious literary, artistic, political, or scientific value" - critically limits the uncertain sweep of the obscenity definition. The second requirement is particularly important because, unlike the "patently offensive" and "prurient interest" criteria, it is not judged by contemporary community standards. This "societal value" requirement, absent in the CDA, allows appellate courts to impose some limitations and regularity on the definition by setting, as a matter of law, a national floor for socially redeeming value. The Government's contention that courts will be able to give such legal limitations to the CDA's standards is belied by *Miller*'s own rationale for having juries determine whether material is "patently offensive" according to community standards - that such questions are essentially ones of fact.

In contrast to *Miller* and our other previous cases, the CDA thus presents a greater threat of censoring speech that, in fact, falls outside the statute's scope. Given the vague contours of the coverage of the statute, it unquestionably silences some speakers whose messages would be entitled to constitutional protection. That danger provides further reason for insisting that the statute not be overly broad. The CDA's burden on protected speech cannot be justified if it could be avoided by a more carefully drafted statute.

We are persuaded that the CDA lacks the precision that the First Amendment requires when a statute regulates the content of speech. In order to deny minors access to potentially harmful speech, the CDA effectively suppresses a large amount of speech that adults have a constitutional right to receive and to address to one another. That burden on adult speech is unacceptable if less restrictive alternatives would be at least as effective in achieving the legitimate purpose that the statute was enacted to serve.

In evaluating the free speech rights of adults, we have made it perfectly clear that "[s]exual expression which is indecent but not obscene is protected by the First Amendment." Indeed, *Pacifica* itself admonished that "the fact that society may find speech offensive is not a sufficient reason for suppressing it."

It is true that we have repeatedly recognized the governmental interest in protecting children from harmful materials. But that interest does not justify an unnecessarily broad suppression of speech addressed to adults. As we have explained, the Government may not "reduc[e] the adult population . . . to . . . only what is fit for children." "[R]egardless of the strength of the government's interest" in protecting children, "[t]he level of discourse reaching a mailbox simply cannot be limited to that which would be suitable for a sandbox."

The District Court was correct to conclude that the CDA effectively resembles the ban on "dial-a-porn" invalidated in *Sable*. In *Sable*, this Court rejected the argument that we should defer to the congressional judgment that nothing less than a total ban would be effective in preventing enterprising youngsters from gaining access to indecent communications. *Sable* thus made clear that the mere fact that a statutory regulation of speech was enacted for the important purpose of protecting children from exposure to sexually explicit material does not foreclose inquiry into its validity. As we pointed out last Term [in *Denver*], that inquiry embodies an "over-arching commitment" to make sure that Congress has designed its statute to accomplish its purpose "without imposing an unnecessarily great restriction on speech."

In arguing that the CDA does not so diminish adult communication, the Government relies on the incorrect factual premise that prohibiting a transmission whenever it is known that one of its recipients is a minor would not interfere with adult-to-adult communication. The findings of the District Court make clear that this premise is untenable. Given the size of the potential audience for most messages, in the absence of a viable age verification process, the sender must be charged with knowing that one or more minors will likely view it. Knowledge that, for instance, one or more members of a 100-person chat group will be minor - and therefore that it would be a crime to send the group an indecent message - would surely burden communication among adults.

The District Court found that at the time of trial existing technology did not include any effective method for a sender to prevent minors from obtaining access to its communications on the Internet without also denying access to adults. The Court found no effective way to determine the age of a user who is accessing material through e-mail, mail exploders, newsgroups, or chat rooms. As a practical matter, the Court also found that it would be prohibitively expensive for noncommercial - as well as some commercial - speakers who have Web sites to verify that their users are adults. These limitations must inevitably curtail a significant amount of adult communication on the Internet. By contrast, the District Court found that "[d]espite its limitations, currently available user-based software suggests that a reasonably effective method by which parents can prevent their children from accessing sexually explicit and other material which parents may believe is inappropriate for their children will soon be widely available."

The breadth of the CDA's coverage is wholly unprecedented. Unlike the regulations upheld in *Ginsberg* and *Pacifica*, the scope of the CDA is not limited to commercial speech or commercial entities. Its open-ended prohibitions embrace all nonprofit entities and individuals posting indecent messages or displaying them on their own computers in the presence of minors. The general, undefined terms "indecent" and "patently offensive" cover large amounts of nonpornographic material with serious educational or other value. Moreover, the "community standards" criterion as applied to the Internet means that any communication available to a nationwide audience will be judged by the standards of the community most likely to be offended by the message. The regulated subject matter includes any of the seven "dirty words" used in the *Pacifica* monologue, the use of which the Government's expert acknowledged could constitute a felony. It may also extend to discussions about prison rape or safe sexual practices, artistic images that include nude subjects, and arguably the card catalog of the Carnegie Library.

For the purposes of our decision, we need neither accept nor reject the Government's submission that the First Amendment does not forbid a blanket prohibition on all "indecent" and "patently offensive" messages communicated to a 17-year-old - no matter how much value the message may contain and regardless of parental approval. It is at least clear that the strength of the Government's interest in protecting minors is not equally strong throughout the coverage of this broad statute. Under the CDA, a parent allowing her 17-year-old to use the family computer to obtain information on the Internet that she, in her parental judgment, deems appropriate, could face a lengthy prison term. Similarly, a parent who sent his 17-year-old college freshman information on birth control via e-mail could be incarcerated even though neither he, his child, nor anyone in their home community, found the material "indecent" or "patently offensive," if the college town's community thought otherwise.

The breadth of this content-based restriction of speech imposes an especially heavy burden on the Government to explain why a less restrictive provision would not be as effective as the CDA. It has not done so. The arguments in this Court have referred to possible alternatives such as requiring that indecent material be "tagged" in a way that facilitates parental control of material coming into their homes, making exceptions for messages with artistic or educational value, providing some tolerance for parental choice, and regulating some portions of the Internet - such as commercial web sites - differently than others, such as chat rooms. Particularly in the light of the absence of any detailed findings by the Congress, or even hearings addressing the special problems of the CDA, we are persuaded that the CDA is not narrowly tailored if that requirement has any meaning at all.

. . . [T]he Government advances three additional arguments for sustaining the Act's affirmative prohibitions:

> (1) that the CDA is constitutional because it leaves open ample "alternative channels" of communication; (2) that the plain meaning of the Act's "knowledge" and "specific person" requirement significantly restricts its permissible applications; and (3) that the Act's prohibitions are "almost always" limited to material lacking redeeming social value.

The Government first contends that, even though the CDA effectively censors discourse on many of the Internet's modalities - such as chat groups, newsgroups, and mail exploders - it is nonetheless constitutional because it provides a "reasonable opportunity" for speakers to engage in the restricted speech on the World Wide Web. . . . The Government's position is equivalent to arguing that a statute could ban leaflets on certain subjects as long as individuals are free to publish books. In invalidating a number of laws that banned leafletting on the streets regardless of their content - we explained that "one is not to have the exercise of his liberty of expression in appropriate places abridged on the plea that it may be exercised in some other place."

The Government also asserts that the "knowledge" requirement . . . , especially when coupled with the "specific child" element . . . , saves the CDA from overbreadth. Because both sections prohibit the dissemination of indecent messages only to persons known to be under 18, the Government argues, it does not require transmitters to "refrain from communicating indecent material to adults; they need only refrain from disseminating such materials to persons they know to be under 18."

This argument ignores the fact that most Internet for[ums] - including chat rooms, newsgroups, mail exploders, and the Web - are open to all comers. . . . Even the strongest reading of the "specific person" requirement . . . cannot save the statute. It would confer broad powers of censorship, in the form of a "heckler's veto," upon any opponent of indecent speech who might simply log on and inform the would-be discoursers that his 17-year-old child - a "specific person . . . under 18 years of age" - would be present.

Finally, we find no textual support for the Government's submission that material having scientific, educational, or other redeeming social value will necessarily fall outside the CDA's "patently offensive" and "indecent" prohibitions.

The Government [has] three remaining arguments. . . . First, relying on the "good faith, reasonable, effective, and appropriate actions" provision, the Government suggests that "tagging" provides a defense that saves the constitutionality of the Act. The suggestion assumes that transmitters may encode their indecent communications in a way that would indicate their contents, thus permitting recipients to block their reception with appropriate software. It is the requirement that the good faith action must be "effective" that makes this defense illusory. The Government recognizes that its proposed screening software does not currently exist. Even if it did, there is no way to know whether a potential recipient will actually block the encoded material. Without the impossible knowledge that every guardian in America is screening for the "tag," the transmitter could not reasonably rely on its action to be "effective."

. . . [W]e can consider [the Government's second and third arguments] together. . . . . [This occurs] when the transmitter has restricted access by requiring use of a verified credit card or adult identification. Such verification is not only technologically available but actually is used by commercial providers of sexually explicit material. These providers, therefore, would be protected by the defense. Under the findings of the District Court, however, it is not economically feasible for most noncommercial speakers to employ such verification. Accordingly, this defense would not significantly narrow the statute's burden on noncommercial speech. Even with respect to the commercial pornographers that would be protected by the defense, the Government failed to adduce [introduce] any evidence that these verification techniques actually preclude minors from posing as adults. Given that the risk of criminal sanctions "hovers over each content provider, like the proverbial sword of Damocles," the District Court correctly refused to rely on unproven future technology to save the statute. The Government thus failed to prove that the proffered defense would significantly reduce the heavy burden on adult speech produced by the prohibition on offensive displays.

We agree with the District Court's conclusion that the CDA places an unacceptably heavy burden on protected speech, and that the defenses do not constitute the sort of "narrow tailoring" that will save an otherwise patently invalid unconstitutional provision. In *Sable*, we remarked that the speech restriction at issue there amounted to "'burn[ing] the house to roast the pig.'" The CDA, casting a far darker shadow over free speech, threatens to torch a large segment of the Internet community.

. . . . The record demonstrates that the growth of the Internet has been and continues to be phenomenal. As a matter of constitutional tradition, in the absence of evidence to the contrary, we presume that governmental regulation of the content of speech is more likely to interfere with the free exchange of ideas than to encourage it. The interest in encouraging freedom of expression in a democratic society outweighs any theoretical but unproven benefit of censorship.

For the foregoing reasons, the judgment of the District Court is affirmed.

X-Rated Cable Broadcasts
Denver Telecommunications v. FCC

Cable operators shall be permitted to prohibit programming that the cable operator reasonably believes to describe or depict sexual activities in a patently offensive manner as measured by contemporary community standards. **- The Federal Cable Act (1992)**

On October 5, 1992, in an effort to protect children from viewing sexually explicit broadcasts over both leased access and public access cable channels, Congress passed the Cable Television Consumer Protection Act. Three provisions of the Cable Act sought to regulate the broadcasting of sexually-oriented material on those two types of cable channels. The first two provisions allowed cable operators to prohibit programming (on either leased or public access channels) that the cable operator believed to be sexually offensive as measured by contemporary community standards. The third provision required the cable operator to segregate, onto a single channel, any remaining sexually-oriented programming and to block that channel unless a viewer requested access in advance and in writing.

The Federal Communications Commission, charged with the enforcement of the Cable Act, issued regulations. Several affected groups representing leased and public access channels (including Denver Educational Television and the Alliance for Community Media) challenged the FCC's regulations as a violation of their First Amendment rights. On June 6, 1995 the U.S. Court of Appeals held that all three provisions were consistent with the First Amendment. Denver Telecommunications and the Alliance for Community Media appealed for a reversal to the United States Supreme Court.

On June 28, 1996 the 6-3 decision of the Court was announced by Associate Justice Stephen Breyer.

The *X-Rated Cable* Court

Chief Justice William Rehnquist
Appointed Chief Justice by President Reagan
Appointed Associate Justice by President Nixon
Served 1971 -

Associate Justice John Paul Stevens
Appointed by President Ford
Served 1975 -

Associate Justice Sandra Day O'Connor
Appointed by President Reagan
Served 1981 -

Associate Justice Antonin Scalia
Appointed by President Reagan
Served 1986 -

Associate Justice Anthony Kennedy
Appointed by President Reagan
Served 1988 -

Associate Justice David Souter
Appointed by President Bush
Served 1990 -

Associate Justice Clarence Thomas
Appointed by President Bush
Served 1991 -

Associate Justice Ruth Bader Ginsberg
Appointed by President Clinton
Served 1993 -

Associate Justice Stephen Breyer
Appointed by President Clinton
Served 1994 -

The unedited text of *Denver Telecommunications v. FCC* can be found in volume 518 of *United States Reports*. Our edited plain-English text follows.

DENVER TELECOMMUNICATIONS
v. FCC
June 28, 1996

JUSTICE STEPHEN BREYER: These cases present First Amendment challenges to three statutory provisions [of the Federal Cable Act of 1992] that seek to regulate the broadcasting of "patently offensive" sex-related material on cable television. The provisions apply to programs broadcast over cable on what are known as "leased access channels" and "public, educational, or governmental channels." Two of the provisions essentially permit a cable system operator to prohibit the broadcasting of "programming" that the "operator reasonably believes describes or depicts sexual or excretory activities or organs in a patently offensive manner." The remaining provision requires cable system operators to segregate certain "patently offensive" programming, to place it on a single channel, and to block that channel from viewer access unless the viewer requests access in advance and in writing.

We conclude that the first provision - that permits the operator to decide whether or not to broadcast such programs on leased access channels - is consistent with the First Amendment. The second provision - that requires leased channel operators to segregate and to block that programming - and the third provision - applicable to public, educational, and governmental channels - violate the First Amendment, for they are not appropriately tailored to achieve the basic, legitimate objective of protecting children from exposure to "patently offensive" material.

Cable operators typically own a physical cable network used to convey programming over several dozen cable channels into subscribers' houses. Program sources vary from channel to channel. Most channels carry programming produced by independent firms, including "many national and regional cable programming networks that have emerged in recent years," as well as some programming that the system operator itself (or an operator affiliate) may provide. Other channels may simply retransmit through cable the signals of over-the-air broadcast stations. Certain special channels here at issue, called "leased channels" and "public, educational, or governmental channels," carry programs provided by those to whom the law gives special cable system access rights.

A "leased channel" is a channel that federal law requires a cable system operator to reserve for commercial lease by unaffiliated third parties. About ten to fifteen percent of a cable system's channels would typically fall into this category. "[P]ublic, educational, or governmental channels" (which we shall call "public access channels") are channels that, over the years, local governments have required cable system operators to set aside for public, educational, or governmental purposes as part of the consideration an operator gives in return for permission to install cables under city streets and to use public rights-of-way. Between 1984 and 1992 federal law (as had much pre-1984 state law, in respect to public access channels) prohibited cable system operators from exercising any editorial control over the content of any program broadcast over either leased or public access channels.

In 1992, in an effort to control sexually explicit programming conveyed over access channels, Congress enacted the three provisions before us. The first two provisions relate to leased channels. The first [Section 10(a)] says, "This subsection shall permit a cable operator to enforce prospectively a written and published policy of prohibiting programming that the cable operator reasonably believes describes or depicts sexual or excretory activities or organs in a patently offensive manner as measured by contemporary community standards."

The second provision [Section 10(b)], applicable only to leased channels, requires cable operators to segregate and to block similar programming if they decide to permit, rather than to prohibit, its broadcast. The provision tells the Federal Communications Commission (FCC) to promulgate regulations that will . . . (a) require "programmers to inform cable operators if the program[ming] would be indecent as defined by Commission regulations"; . . . (b) require "cable operators to place" such material "on a single channel"; and . . . (c) require "cable operators to block such single channel unless the subscriber requests access to such channel in writing."

The third provision [Section 10(c)] is similar to the first provision, but applies only to public access channels. The relevant statutory section instructs the FCC to promulgate regulations that will "enable a cable operator of a cable system to prohibit the use, on such system, of any channel capacity of any public, educational, or governmental access facility for any programming which contains obscene material, sexually explicit conduct, or material soliciting or promoting unlawful conduct."

. . . . [T]he federal law before us . . . now permits cable operators either to allow or to forbid the transmission of "patently offensive" sex-related materials over both leased and public access channels, and requires those operators, at a minimum, to segregate and to block transmission of that same material on leased channels.

Petitioners [Denver Telecommunications], claiming that the three statutory provisions, as implemented by the Commission regulations, violate the First Amendment, sought judicial review . . . in the United States Court of Appeals for the

District of Columbia Circuit. A panel of that Circuit agreed with [Denver Telecommunications] that the provisions violated the First Amendment. The entire Court of Appeals, however, heard the case en banc [with all its members] and reached the opposite conclusion. . . . We granted certiorari [agreed to hear the case] to review the en banc Court's First Amendment determinations.

We turn initially to the provision that permits cable system operators to prohibit "patently offensive" (or "indecent") programming transmitted over leased access channels. . . .

We recognize that the First Amendment, the terms of which apply to governmental action, ordinarily does not itself throw into constitutional doubt the decisions of private citizens to permit, or to restrict, speech - and this is so ordinarily even where those decisions take place within the framework of a regulatory regime such as broadcasting. Were that not so, courts might have to face the difficult, and potentially restrictive, practical task of deciding which, among any number of private parties involved in providing a program (for example, networks, station owners, program editors, and program producers), is the "speaker" whose rights may not be abridged, and who is the speech-restricting "censor." Furthermore, as this Court has held, the editorial function itself is an aspect of "speech," and a court's decision that a private party, say, the station owner, is a "censor," could itself interfere with that private "censor's" freedom to speak as an editor. Thus, not surprisingly, this Court's First Amendment broadcasting cases have dealt with governmental efforts to restrict, not governmental efforts to provide or to maintain, a broadcaster's freedom to pick and to choose programming.

Nonetheless, [Denver Telecommunications], while conceding that this is ordinarily so, point[s] to circumstances that, in their view, make the analogy with private broadcasters inapposite and make this case a special one, warranting a different constitutional result. As a practical matter, they say, cable system operators have considerably more power to "censor" program viewing than do broadcasters, for individual communities typically have only one cable system, linking broadcasters and other program providers with each community's many subscribers. Moreover, concern about system operators' exercise of this considerable power originally led government - local and federal - to insist that operators provide leased and public access channels free of operator editorial control. To permit system operators to supervise programming on leased access channels will create the very private-censorship risk that this anti-censorship effort sought to avoid. At the same time, [Denver Telecommunications] add[s], cable systems have two relevant special characteristics. They are unusually involved with government, for they depend upon government permission and government facilities (streets, rights-of-way) to string the cable necessary for their services. And in respect to leased channels, their speech interests are relatively weak because they act less like editors, such as newspapers or television broadcasters, than like common carriers, such as telephone companies.

Under these circumstances, [Denver Telecommunications] conclude[s], Congress' "permissive law," in actuality, will abridge their free speech. And this Court should treat that law as a congressionally imposed, content-based restriction, unredeemed as a properly tailored effort to serve a "compelling interest." . . .

The history of this Court's First Amendment jurisprudence [philosophy of law], however, is one of continual development, as the Constitution's general command that "Congress shall make no law . . . abridging the freedom of speech, or of the press," has been applied to new circumstances requiring different adaptations of prior principles and precedents. The essence of that protection is that Congress may not regulate speech except in cases of extraordinary need and with the exercise of a degree of care that we have not elsewhere required. At the same time, our cases have not left Congress or the States powerless to address the most serious problems.

Over the years, this Court has restated and refined these basic First Amendment principles, adopting them more particularly to the balance of competing interests and the special circumstances of each field of application.

This tradition teaches that the First Amendment embodies an overarching commitment to protect speech from Government regulation through close judicial scrutiny, thereby enforcing the Constitution's constraints, but without imposing judicial formula[s] so rigid that they become a straightjacket that disables Government from responding to serious problems. This Court, in different contexts, has consistently held that the Government may directly regulate speech to address extraordinary problems, where its regulations are appropriately tailored to resolve those problems without imposing an unnecessarily great restriction on speech. . . .

First, the provision before us comes accompanied with an extremely important justification, one that this Court has often found compelling - the need to protect children from exposure to patently offensive sex-related material.

Second, the provision arises in a very particular context - congressional permission for cable operators to regulate programming that, but for a previous Act of Congress, would have had no path of access to cable channels free of an operator's control. The First Amendment interests involved are therefore complex, and involve a balance between those interests served by the access requirements themselves (increasing the availability of avenues of expression to programmers who otherwise would not have them), and the disadvantage to the First Amendment interests of cable operators and other programmers (those to whom the cable operator would have assigned the channels devoted to access).

Third, the problem Congress addressed here is remarkably similar to the problem addressed by the FCC in *Pacifica*, and the balance Congress struck is commensurate with the balance we approved there. . . .

All these factors are present here. Cable television broadcasting, including access channel broadcasting, is as "accessible to children" as over-the-air broadcasting, if not more so. Cable television systems, including access channels, "have established a uniquely pervasive presence in the lives of all Americans." "Patently offensive" material from these stations can "confron[t] the citizen" in the "privacy of the home," with little or no prior warning. There is nothing to stop "adults who feel the need" from finding similar programming elsewhere, say, on tape or in theaters. In fact, the power of cable systems to control home program viewing is not absolute. Over-the-air broadcasting and direct broadcast satellites already provide alternative ways for programmers to reach the home, and are likely to do so to a greater extent in the near future.

Fourth, the permissive nature of Section 10(a) means that it likely restricts speech less than, not more than, the ban at issue in *Pacifica*. The provision removes a restriction as to some speakers - namely, cable operators. Moreover, although the provision does create a risk that a program will not appear, that risk is not the same as the certainty that accompanies a governmental ban. In fact, a glance at the programming that cable operators allow on their own (nonaccess) channels suggests that this distinction is not theoretical, but real. Finally, the provision's permissive nature brings with it a flexibility that allows cable operators, for example, not to ban broadcasts, but, say, to rearrange broadcast times, better to fit the desires of adult audiences while lessening the risks of harm to children. In all these respects, the permissive nature of the approach taken by Congress renders this measure appropriate as a means of achieving the underlying purpose of protecting children.

Of course, cable system operators may not always rearrange or reschedule patently offensive programming. Sometimes, as [Denver Telecommunications] fear[s], they may ban the programming instead. But the same may be said of *Pacifica*'s ban. In practice, the FCC's daytime broadcast ban could have become a total ban, depending upon how private operators (programmers, station owners, networks) responded to it. They would have had to decide whether to reschedule the daytime show for nighttime broadcast in light of comparative audience demand and a host of other practical factors that similarly would determine the practical outcomes of the provisions before us. The upshot, in both cases, must be uncertainty as to practical consequences - of the governmental ban in the one case and of the permission in the other. . . .

The existence of this complex balance of interests persuades us that the permissive nature of the provision, coupled with its viewpoint-neutral application, is a constitutionally permissible way to protect children from the type of sexual material that concerned Congress, while accommodating both the First Amendment interests served by the access requirements and those served in restoring to cable operators a degree of the editorial control that Congress removed in 1984.

. . . . [A]s this Court pointed out in *Pacifica*, what is "patently offensive" depends on context (the kind of program on which it appears), degree (not "an occasional expletive"), and time of broadcast (a "pig" is offensive in "the parlor" but not the "barnyard"). Programming at two o'clock in the morning is seen by a basically adult audience and the "patently offensive" must be defined with that fact in mind.

. . . . [W]e conclude that Section 10(a) is consistent with the First Amendment.

The statute's second provision significantly differs from the first, for it does not simply permit, but rather requires, cable system operators to restrict speech - by segregating and blocking "patently offensive" sex-related material appearing on leased channels (but not on other channels). In particular, . . . this provision and its implementing regulations require cable system operators to place "patently offensive" leased channel programming on a separate channel; to block that channel; to unblock the channel within thirty days of a subscriber's written request for access; and to reblock the channel within thirty days of a subscriber's request for reblocking. Also, leased channel programmers must notify cable operators of an intended "patently offensive" broadcast up to thirty days before its scheduled broadcast date.

These requirements have obvious restrictive effects. The several up-to-thirty-day delays, along with single channel segregation, mean that a subscriber cannot decide to watch a single program without considerable advance planning and without letting the "patently offensive" channel in its entirety invade his household for days, perhaps weeks, at a time. These restrictions will prevent programmers from broadcasting to viewers who select programs day by day (or, through "surfing," minute by minute); to viewers who would like occasionally to watch a few, but not many, of the programs on the "patently offensive" channel; and to viewers who simply tend to judge a program's value through channel reputation, i.e., by the company it keeps. Moreover, the "written notice" requirement will further restrict viewing by subscribers who fear for their reputations should the operator, advertently or inadvertently, disclose the list of those who wish to watch the "patently offensive" channel. Further, the added costs and burdens that these requirements impose upon a cable system operator may encourage that operator to ban programming that the operator would otherwise permit to run, even if only late at night.

The Government argues that, despite these adverse consequences, the "segregate and block" requirements are lawful because they are "the least restrictive means of realizing" a "compelling interest," namely "protecting the physical and psychological well-being of minors." It adds that, in any event, the First Amendment, as applied in *Pacifica*, "does not require that regulations of indecency on television be subject to the strictest" First Amendment "standard of review."

We agree with the Government that protection of children is a "compelling interest." But we do not agree that the "segregate and block" requirements properly accommodate the speech restrictions they impose and the legitimate objective they seek to attain. . . .

Several circumstances lead us to this conclusion. For one thing, the law, as recently amended, uses other means to protect children from similar "patently offensive" material broadcast on unleased cable channels, i.e., broadcast over any of a system's numerous ordinary, or public access, channels. The law, as recently amended, requires cable operators to "scramble or . . . block" such programming on any (unleased) channel "primarily dedicated to sexually-oriented programming." In addition, cable operators must honor a subscriber's request to block any, or all, programs on any channel to which he or she does not wish to subscribe. And manufacturers, in the future, will have to make television sets with a so-called "V chip" - a device that will be able automatically to identify and block sexually explicit or violent programs.

. . . . [T]he new provisions . . . do not force the viewer to receive (for days or weeks at a time) all "patently offensive" programming or none; they will not lead the viewer automatically to judge the few by the reputation of the many; and they will not automatically place the occasional viewer's name on a special list. They therefore inevitably lead us to ask why, if they adequately protect children from "patently offensive" material broadcast on ordinary channels, they would not offer adequate protection from similar leased channel broadcasts as well? Alternatively, if these provisions do not adequately protect children from patently offensive material broadcast on ordinary channels, how could one justify more severe leased channel restrictions when (given ordinary channel programming) they would yield so little additional protection for children?

. . . . We recognize, as the Solicitor General properly points out, that Congress need not deal with every problem at once; and Congress also must have a degree of leeway in tailoring means to ends. But in light of the 1996 statute, it seems fair to say that Congress now has tried to deal with most of the problem. At this point, we can take Congress' different, and significantly less restrictive, treatment of a highly similar problem at least as some indication that more restrictive means are not "essential" (or will not prove very helpful).

The record's description [in this case] and discussion of a different alternative, the "lockbox," leads, through a different route, to a similar conclusion. The Cable Communications Policy Act of 1984 required cable operators to provide "upon the request of a subscriber, a device by which the subscriber can prohibit viewing of a particular cable service during periods selected by the subscriber."

This device - the "lockbox" - would help protect children by permitting their parents to "lock out" those programs or channels that they did not want their children to see. The FCC, in upholding the "segregate and block" provisions, said that lockboxes protected children (including, say, children with inattentive parents) less effectively than those provisions. But it is important to understand why that is so.

The Government sets forth the reasons as follows, "In the case of lockboxes, parents would have to discover that such devices exist; find out that their cable operators offer them for sale; spend the time and money to buy one; learn how to program the lockbox to block undesired programs; and, finally, exercise sufficient vigilance to ensure that they have, indeed, locked out whatever indecent programming they do not wish their children to view."

We assume the accuracy of this statement. But, the reasons do not show need for a provision as restrictive as the one before us. Rather, they suggest a set of provisions very much like those that Congress [enacted].

No provision, we concede, short of an absolute ban, can offer certain protection against assault by a determined child. We have not, however, generally allowed this fact alone to justify "reduc[ing] the adult population . . . to . . . only what is fit for children." But, leaving that problem aside, the Solicitor General's list of practical difficulties would seem to call, not for "segregate and block" requirements, but, rather, for informational requirements, for a simple coding system, for readily available blocking equipment (perhaps accessible by telephone), for imposing cost burdens upon system operators (who may spread them through subscription fees); or perhaps even for a system that requires lockbox defaults to be set to block certain channels (say, sex-dedicated channels). These kinds of requirements resemble those that Congress has recently imposed upon all but leased channels. For that reason, the "lockbox description" and the discussion of its frailties reinforces our conclusion that the leased channel provision is overly restrictive when measured against the benefits it is likely to achieve. (We add that the record's discussion of the "lockbox" does not explain why the law now treats leased channels more restrictively than ordinary channels.)

There may, of course, be other explanations. Congress may simply not have bothered to change the leased channel provisions when it introduced a new system for other channels. But responses of this sort, like guesses about the comparative seriousness of the problem, are not legally adequate. In other cases, where, as here, the record before Congress or before an agency provides no convincing explanation, this Court has not been willing to stretch the limits of the plausible, to create hypothetical nonobvious explanations in order to justify laws that impose significant restrictions upon speech.

Consequently, we cannot find that the "segregate and block" restrictions on speech are a narrowly, or reasonably, tailored effort to protect children. Rather, they are overly restrictive, "sacrific[ing]" important First Amendment interests for too "speculative a gain." For that reason they are not consistent with the First Amendment.

The statute's third provision, as implemented by FCC regulation, is similar to its first provision, in that it too permits a cable operator to prevent transmission of "patently offensive" programming, in this case on public access channels. But there are four important differences.

The first is the historical background. . . . [C]able operators have traditionally agreed to reserve channel capacity for public, governmental, and educational channels as part of the consideration they give municipalities that award them cable franchises. . . . [T]he requirement to reserve capacity for public access channels is similar to the reservation of a public easement, or a dedication of land for streets and parks, as part of a municipality's approval of a subdivision of land. Significantly, these are channels over which cable operators have not historically exercised editorial control. Unlike Section 10(a) therefore, Section 10(c) does not restore to cable operators editorial rights that they once had, and the countervailing First Amendment interest is nonexistent, or at least much diminished.

The second difference is the institutional background that has developed as a result of the historical difference. When a "leased channel" is made available by the operator to a private lessee, the lessee has total control of programming during the leased time slot. Public access channels, on the other hand, are normally subject to complex supervisory systems of various sorts, often with both public and private elements. Municipalities generally provide in their cable franchising agreements for an access channel manager, who is most commonly a nonprofit organization, but may also be the municipality, or, in some instances, the cable system owner. Access channel activity and management are partly financed with public funds - through franchise fees or other payments pursuant to the franchise agreement, or from general municipal funds.

This system of public, private, and mixed nonprofit elements, through its supervising boards and nonprofit or governmental access managers, can set programming policy and approve or disapprove particular programming services. And this system can police that policy by, for example, requiring indemnification by programmers, certification of compliance with local standards, time segregation, adult content advisories, or even by prescreening individual programs. Whether these locally accountable bodies prescreen programming, promulgate rules for the use of public access channels, or are merely available to respond when problems arise, the upshot is the same - there is a locally accountable body capable of addressing the problem, should it arise, of patently offensive programming broadcast to children, making it unlikely that many children will in fact be exposed to programming considered patently offensive in that community.

Third, the existence of a system aimed at encouraging and securing programming that the community considers valuable strongly suggests that a "cable operator's veto" is less likely necessary to achieve the statute's basic objective, protecting children, than a similar veto in the context of leased channels. Of course, the system of access managers and supervising boards can make mistakes, which the operator might in some cases correct with its veto power. Balanced against this potential benefit, however, is the risk that the veto itself may be mistaken; and its use, or threatened use, could prevent the presentation of programming, that, though borderline, is not "patently offensive" to its targeted audience. And this latter threat must bulk large within a system that already has publicly accountable systems for maintaining responsible programs.

Finally, our examination of the legislative history and the record before us is consistent with what common sense suggests, namely that the public/nonprofit programming control systems now in place would normally avoid, minimize, or eliminate any child-related problems concerning "patently offensive" programming. We have found anecdotal references to what seem isolated instances of potentially indecent programming, some of which may well have occurred on leased, not public access, channels.

But these few examples do not necessarily indicate a significant nationwide pattern. The Commission itself did not report any examples of "indecent programs" on public access channels. Moreover, comments submitted to the FCC undermine any suggestion that prior to 1992 there were significant problems of indecent programming on public access channels.

At most, we have found borderline examples as to which people's judgment may differ, perhaps acceptable in some communities but not others, of the type that [Denver Telecommunications] fear[s] the law might prohibit. It is difficult to see how such borderline examples could show a compelling need, nationally, to protect children from significantly harmful materials. In the absence of a factual basis substantiating the harm and the efficacy of its proposed cure, we cannot assume that the harm exists or that the regulation redresses it.

The upshot, in respect to the public access channels, is a law that could radically change present programming-related relationships among local community and nonprofit supervising boards and access managers, which relationships are established through municipal law, regulation, and contract. In doing so, it would not significantly restore editorial rights of cable operators, but would greatly increase the risk that certain categories of programming (say, borderline offensive programs) will not appear. At the same time, given present supervisory mechanisms, the need for this particular provision, aimed directly at public access channels, is not obvious. Having carefully reviewed the legislative history of the Act, the proceedings before the FCC, the record [of the lower court], and the submissions of the parties and amici [friends of the Court] here, we conclude that the Government cannot sustain [maintain] its burden of showing that Section 10(c) is necessary to protect children or that it is appropriately tailored to secure that end.

For these reasons, the judgment of the Court of Appeals is affirmed [upheld] insofar as it upheld Section 10(a); the judgment of the Court of Appeals is reversed insofar as it upheld Sections 10(b) and 10(c).

The Striptease
Barnes v. Glen Theatre

A person who knowingly or intentionally, in a public place, appears in a state of nudity, commits public indecency, a misdemeanor.
- Indiana's Public Indecency Law (1988)

South Bend, Indiana police raided two adult strip clubs, the Kitty Kat Lounge, a "go-go bar" offering on-stage, semi-nude female dancers, and the Glen Theatre, an adult book-store offering pay-per-view "peep-shows" of semi-nude female dancers. The strip club owners joined with several of their female dancers to bring suit in Federal Court against the enforcement of the provisions of Indiana's Public Inde-cency Law. They claimed the law's prohibition of a strip-tease ending in totally nudity violated their First Amend-ment right to "free expression."

On September 9, 1988 the U.S. District Court held that In-diana's Public Indecency Law was not a violation of either the owners' or the dancers' constitutional rights. The Court found that non-obscene striptease ending in totally nudity performed for entertainment purposes was not "an expres-sive activity" protected by the First Amendment. The own-ers and dancers appealed for a reversal to the U.S. Court of Appeals.

On January 8, 1990 the U.S. Court of Appeals reversed the decision of the District Court, finding that such a striptease performed for entertainment purposes was "an expressive activity" protected by the First Amendment and that Indi-ana's Public Indecency Law was an unconstitutional in-fringement on the dancers' "message of eroticism and sexuality." Indiana's St. Joseph County Prosecuting Attor-ney, Michael Barnes, appealed for a reversal of this decision to the United States Supreme Court.

On June 21, 1991 the 5-4 decision of the Court was an-nounced by Chief Justice William Rehnquist.

The *Striptease* Court

Chief Justice William Rehnquist
Appointed Chief Justice by President Reagan
Appointed Associate Justice by President Nixon
Served 1971 -

Associate Justice Byron White
Appointed by President Kennedy
Served 1962 - 1993

Associate Justice Thurgood Marshall
Appointed by President Lyndon Johnson
Served 1967 - 1991

Associate Justice Harry Blackmun
Appointed by President Nixon
Served 1970 - 1994

Associate Justice John Paul Stevens
Appointed by President Ford
Served 1975 -

Associate Justice Sandra Day O'Connor
Appointed by President Reagan
Served 1981 -

Associate Justice Antonin Scalia
Appointed by President Reagan
Served 1986 -

Associate Justice Anthony Kennedy
Appointed by President Reagan
Served 1988 -

Associate Justice David Souter
Appointed by President Bush
Served 1990 -

The unedited text of *Barnes v. Glen Theatre* can be found in volume 501 of *United States Reports*. Our edited plain-English text follows.

BARNES v. GLEN THEATRE
June 21, 1991

CHIEF JUSTICE WILLIAM REHNQUIST: Respondents are two establishments in South Bend, Indiana, that wish to provide totally nude dancing as entertainment, and individual dancers who are employed at these establishments. They claim that the First Amendment's guarantee of freedom of expression prevents the State of Indiana from enforcing its public indecency law to prevent this form of dancing. We reject their claim.

The facts appear from the pleadings and findings of the District Court and are uncontested here. The Kitty Kat Lounge, Inc. (Kitty Kat), is located in the city of South Bend. It sells alcoholic beverages and presents "go-go dancing." Its proprietor desires to present "totally nude dancing," but an applicable Indiana statute regulating public nudity requires that the dancers wear "pasties" and "G-strings" when they dance. The dancers are not paid an hourly wage, but work on commission. They receive a 100 percent commission on the first $60 in drink sales during their performances. Darlene Miller, one of the respondents in the action, had worked at the Kitty Kat for about two years at the time this action was brought. Miller wishes to dance nude because she believes she would make more money doing so.

. . . Glen Theatre, Inc. is an Indiana corporation with a place of business in South Bend. Its primary business is supplying so-called adult entertainment through written and printed materials, movie showings, and live entertainment at an enclosed "bookstore." The live entertainment at the "bookstore" consists of nude and seminude performances and showings of the female body through glass panels. Customers sit in a booth and insert coins into a timing mechanism that permits them to observe the live nude and seminude dancers for a period of time. One of Glen Theatre's dancers, Gayle Ann Marie Sutro, has danced, modeled, and acted professionally for more than fifteen years, and in addition to her performances at the Glen Theatre, can be seen in a pornographic movie at a nearby theater.

[Kitty Kat and Glen Theatre] sued in the United States District Court for the Northern District of Indiana to enjoin [prohibit] the enforcement of the Indiana public indecency statute, asserting that its prohibition against complete nudity in public places violated the First Amendment. The District Court originally granted . . . an injunction [court order stopping an action], finding that the statute was . . . overbroad. The Court of Appeals for the Seventh Circuit reversed. . . and this Court . . . remanded [returned the case] to the District Court . . . for the plaintiffs [Kitty Kat and Glen Theatre] to pursue their claim that the statute violated the First Amendment as applied to their dancing. . . . [T]he District Court concluded that "the type of dancing these plaintiffs wish to perform is not expressive activity protected by the Constitution of the United States," and rendered judgment in favor of the defendants [Michael Barnes, the St. Joseph, Indiana prosecuting attorney]. The case was again appealed to the Seventh Circuit, and a panel of that court reversed the District Court, holding that the nude dancing involved here was expressive conduct protected by the First Amendment. The Court of Appeals then heard the case en banc [by the entire court], and the court rendered a series of comprehensive and thoughtful opinions. The majority concluded that nonobscene nude dancing performed for entertainment is expression protected by the First Amendment, and that the public indecency statute was an improper infringement of that expressive activity because its purpose was to prevent the message of eroticism and sexuality conveyed by the dancers. We granted certiorari [agreed to hear the case] and now hold that the Indiana statutory requirement that the dancers in the establishments involved in this case must wear pasties and G-strings does not violate the First Amendment.

Several of our cases contain language suggesting that nude dancing of the kind involved here is expressive conduct protected by the First Amendment. In *Doran v. Salem*, we said, "[A]lthough the customary 'barroom' type of nude dancing may involve only the barest minimum of protected expression, we recognized in *California v. LaRue* that this form of entertainment might be entitled to First and Fourteenth Amendment protection under some circumstances." In *Schad v. Mount Ephraim*, we said that, "[f]urthermore, as the state courts in this case recognized, nude dancing is not without its First Amendment protections from official regulation." These statements support the conclusion of the Court of Appeals that nude dancing of the kind sought to be performed here is expressive conduct within the outer perimeters of the First Amendment, though we view it as only marginally so. This, of course, does not end our inquiry. We must determine the level of protection to be afforded to the expressive conduct at issue, and must determine whether the Indiana statute is an impermissible infringement of that protected activity.

Indiana, of course, has not banned nude dancing as such, but has proscribed [prohibited] public nudity across the board. The Supreme Court of Indiana has construed [interpreted] the Indiana statute to preclude nudity in what are essentially places of public accommodation such as the Glen Theatre and the Kitty Kat Lounge. In such places, [Kitty Kat and Glen Theatre] point out, minors are excluded and there are no nonconsenting viewers. [They] contend that while the State may license establishments such as the ones involved here, and limit the geographical area in which they do business, it may not in any way limit the performance of the dances within them without violating the First Amendment. [Barnes] contend[s], on the other hand, that Indiana's restriction on nude dancing is a valid "time, place, or manner" restriction. . . .

The "time, place, or manner" test was developed for evaluating restrictions on expression taking place on public property which had been dedicated as a "public forum," although we have on at least one occasion applied it to conduct occurring on private property. In *Clark [v. Commuity for Creative Non-Violence]*, we observed that this test has been interpreted to embody much the same standards as those set forth in *United States v. O'Brien* and we turn, therefore, to the rule enunciated in *O'Brien*.

O'Brien burned his draft card on the steps of the South Boston Courthouse in the presence of a sizable crowd, and was convicted of violating a statute that prohibited the knowing destruction or mutilation of such a card. He claimed that his conviction was contrary to the First Amendment because his act was "symbolic speech" - expressive conduct. The Court rejected his contention that symbolic speech is entitled to full First Amendment protection, saying,

"[E]ven on the assumption that the alleged communicative element in O'Brien's conduct is sufficient to bring into play the First Amendment, it does not necessarily follow that the destruction of a registration certificate is constitutionally protected activity. This Court has held that when 'speech' and 'nonspeech' elements are combined in the same course of conduct, a sufficiently important governmental interest in regulating the nonspeech element can justify incidental limitations on First Amendment freedoms. To characterize the quality of the governmental interest which must appear, the Court has employed a variety of descriptive terms - compelling; substantial; subordinating; paramount; cogent; strong.

Whatever imprecision inheres in these terms, we think it clear that a government regulation is sufficiently justified if it is within the constitutional power of the Government; if it furthers an important or substantial governmental interest; if the governmental interest is unrelated to the suppression of free expression; and if the incidental restriction on alleged First Amendment freedoms is no greater than is essential to the furtherance of that interest."

Applying the four-part *O'Brien* test enunciated above, we find that Indiana's public indecency statute is justified despite its incidental limitations on some expressive activity. The public indecency statute is clearly within the constitutional power of the State and furthers substantial governmental interests. It is impossible to discern, other than from the text of the statute, exactly what governmental interest the Indiana legislators had in mind when they enacted this statute, for Indiana does not record legislative history, and the State's highest court has not shed additional light on the statute's purpose. Nonetheless, the statute's purpose of protecting societal order and morality is clear from its text and history. Public indecency statutes of this sort are of ancient origin and presently exist in at least forty-seven States. Public indecency, including nudity, was a criminal offense at common law, and this Court recognized the common-law roots of the offense of "gross and open indecency." Public nudity was considered an act malum in se [wrong in itself]. Public indecency statutes such as the one before us reflect moral disapproval of people appearing in the nude among strangers in public places.

This public indecency statute follows a long line of earlier Indiana statutes banning all public nudity. The history of Indiana's public indecency statute shows that it predates barroom nude dancing and was enacted as a general prohibition. At least as early as 1831, Indiana had a statute punishing "open and notorious lewdness, or . . . any grossly scandalous and public indecency." A gap during which no statute was in effect was filled by the Indiana Supreme Court in *Ardery v. State*, which held that the court could sustain [uphold] a conviction for exhibition of "privates" in the presence of others. The court traced the offense to the Bible story of Adam and Eve. In 1881 a statute was enacted that would remain essentially unchanged for nearly a century, "Whoever, being over fourteen years of age, makes an indecent exposure of his person in a public place, or in any place where there are other persons to be offended or annoyed thereby, . . . is guilty of public indecency. . . ."

The language quoted above remained unchanged until it was simultaneously repealed and replaced with the present statute in 1976.

This and other public indecency statutes were designed to protect morals and public order. The traditional police power of the States is defined as the authority to provide for the public health, safety, and morals, and we have upheld such a basis for legislation. In *Paris Adult Theatre I v. Slaton*, we said, "In deciding *Roth [v. United States]*, this Court implicitly accepted that a legislature could legitimately act on such a conclusion to protect 'the social interest in order and morality.'"

And in *Bowers v. Hardwick*, we said, "The law, however, is constantly based on notions of morality, and if all laws representing essentially moral choices are to be invalidated under the Due Process Clause, the courts will be very busy indeed." Thus, the public indecency statute furthers a substantial government interest in protecting order and morality.

This interest is unrelated to the suppression of free expression. Some may view restricting nudity on moral grounds as necessarily related to expression. We disagree. It can be argued, of course, that almost limitless types of conduct - including appearing in the nude in public - are "expressive," and in one sense of the word this is true. People who go about in the nude in public may be expressing something about themselves by so doing. But the court rejected this expansive notion of "expressive conduct" in *O'Brien*, saying, "We cannot accept the view that an apparently limitless variety of conduct can be labeled 'speech' whenever the person engaging in the conduct intends thereby to express an idea."

And in *Dallas [v. Stanglin]*, we further observed,

"It is possible to find some kernel of expression in almost every activity a person undertakes - for example, walking down the street or meeting one's friends at a shopping mall - but such a kernel is not sufficient to bring the activity within the protection of the First Amendment. We think the activity of these dancehall patrons - coming together to engage in recreational dancing - is not protected by the First Amendment."

[Kitty Kat and Glen Theatre] contend that even though prohibiting nudity in public generally may not be related to suppressing expression, prohibiting the performance of nude dancing is related to expression because the State seeks to prevent its erotic message. . . .

[W]e do not think that when Indiana applies its statute to the nude dancing in these nightclubs it is proscribing nudity because of the erotic message conveyed by the dancers. Presumably numerous other erotic performances are presented at these establishments and similar clubs without any interference from the State, so long as the performers wear a scant amount of clothing. Likewise, the requirement that the dancers don pasties and G-strings does not deprive the dance of whatever erotic message it conveys; it simply makes the message slightly less graphic. The perceived evil that Indiana seeks to address is not erotic dancing, but public nudity. The appearance of people of all shapes, sizes, and ages in the nude at a beach, for example, would convey little if any erotic message, yet the State still seeks to prevent it. Public nudity is the evil the State seeks to prevent, whether or not it is combined with expressive activity.

This conclusion is buttressed by a reference to the facts of *O'Brien*. An Act of Congress provided that anyone who knowingly destroyed a Selective Service registration certificate committed an offense. O'Brien burned his certificate on the steps of the South Boston Courthouse to influence others to adopt his antiwar beliefs. This Court upheld his conviction, reasoning that the continued availability of issued certificates served a legitimate and substantial purpose in the administration of the Selective Service System. O'Brien's deliberate destruction of his certificate frustrated this purpose and "[f]or this noncommunicative impact of his conduct, and for nothing else, he was convicted." It was assumed that O'Brien's act in burning the certificate had a communicative element in it sufficient to bring into play the First Amendment, but it was for the noncommunicative element that he was prosecuted. So here with the Indiana statute; while the dancing to which it was applied had a communicative element, it was not the dancing that was prohibited, but simply its being done in the nude.

The fourth part of the *O'Brien* test requires that the incidental restriction on First Amendment freedom be no greater than is essential to the furtherance of the governmental interest. As indicated in the discussion above, the governmental interest served by the text of the prohibition is societal disapproval of nudity in public places and among strangers. The statutory prohibition is not a means to some greater end, but an end in itself. It is without cavil that the public indecency statute is "narrowly tailored"; Indiana's requirement that the dancers wear at least pasties and G-strings is modest, and the bare minimum necessary to achieve the State's purpose.

The judgment of the Court of Appeals accordingly is reversed.

"Dial-A-Porn"
Sable Communications v. FCC

In the 1980's "Dial-A-Porn," the commercial provision of prerecorded, sexually-oriented telephone messages, became a multimillion dollar business. Typical messages lasted from 30 seconds to 2 minutes and could be called by up to 50,000 people an hour. Special high-volume "976" phone numbers were assigned by telephone companies to "dial-a-porn" businesses. The profits from these calls, which carried high fees - several dollars per minute - were split by the telephone companies and the "dial-a-porn" businesses. In 1985 it was estimated that between twelve and fourteen million calls were made to New York City's "dial-a-porn" numbers.

On July 1, 1988, in an effort to prevent minors from being able to access sexually-oriented, prerecorded telephone messages, Congress passed the Telephone Decency Act, an amendment to the Federal Communications Act. This "Dial-A-Porn" amendment prohibited, under penalty of law, the provision of "indecent" and/or "obscene" telephone recordings to anyone, regardless of age.

Sable Communications, a major "dial-a-porn" provider, brought suit in U.S. District Court against the Federal Communications Commission (FCC) to stop the enforcement of the "Dial-A-Porn" amendment. Sable challenged the constitutionality of the "Dial-A-Porn" amendment as a violation of their First Amendment "free speech" rights.

The District Court, in a split decision, found that the "obscenity" provisions of the "Dial-A-Porn" amendment were constitutional but that its "indecency" provisions were unconstitutional. Both the FCC and Sable Communications appealed to the United States Supreme Court.

On June 23, 1989 the 6-3 decision of the Court was announced by Associate Justice Byron White.

The *Dial-A-Porn* Court

Chief Justice William Rehnquist
Appointed Chief Justice by President Reagan
Appointed Associate Justice by President Nixon
Served 1971 -

Associate Justice William Brennan
Appointed by President Eisenhower
Served 1956 - 1990

Associate Justice Byron White
Appointed by President Kennedy
Served 1962 - 1993

Associate Justice Thurgood Marshall
Appointed by President Lyndon Johnson
Served 1967 - 1991

Associate Justice Harry Blackmun
Appointed by President Nixon
Served 1970 - 1994

Associate Justice John Paul Stevens
Appointed by President Ford
Served 1975 -

Associate Justice Sandra Day O'Connor
Appointed by President Reagan
Served 1981 -

Associate Justice Antonin Scalia
Appointed by President Reagan
Served 1986 -

Associate Justice Anthony Kennedy
Appointed by President Reagan
Served 1988 -

The unedited text of *Sable Communications v. Federal Communications Commission* can be found in volume 492 of *United States Reports.* Our edited plain-English text follows.

SABLE COMMUNICATIONS v. FCC
June 23, 1989

JUSTICE BYRON WHITE: The issue before us is the constitutionality of Section 223(b) [the Dial-A-Porn Amendment] of the Communications Act of 1934. The statute, as amended in 1988, imposes an outright ban on indecent as well as obscene interstate commercial telephone messages. The District Court upheld the prohibition against obscene interstate telephone communications for commercial purposes, but enjoined [stopped] the enforcement of the statute insofar as it applied to indecent messages. We affirm [uphold] the District Court in both respects.

In 1983, Sable Communications, Inc., a Los Angeles-based affiliate of Carlin Communications, Inc., began offering sexually-oriented, prerecorded telephone messages (popularly known as "dial-a-porn") through the Pacific Bell telephone network. In order to provide the messages, Sable arranged with Pacific Bell to use special telephone lines, designed to handle large volumes of calls simultaneously. Those who called the adult message number were charged a special fee. The fee was collected by Pacific Bell and divided between the phone company and the message provider. Callers outside the Los Angeles metropolitan area could reach the number by means of a long-distance toll call to the Los Angeles area code.

In 1988, Sable brought suit in District Court seeking . . . injunctive relief [a court order stopping an action] against enforcement of the . . . [Dial-A-Porn Amendment]. The 1988 amendments to the statute imposed a blanket prohibition on indecent as well as obscene interstate commercial telephone messages. Sable brought this action to [stop] the FCC and the Justice Department from initiating any criminal investigation or prosecution, civil action or administrative proceeding under the statute. Sable also . . . challeng[ed] the indecency and the obscenity provisions of the . . . [Dial-A-Porn Amendment] as unconstitutional, chiefly under the First and Fourteenth Amendments to the Constitution.

The District Court found that a concrete controversy existed. . . . [They] denied Sable's request for a preliminary injunction against enforcement of the statute's ban on obscene telephone messages, rejecting the argument that the statute was unconstitutional because it created a national standard of obscenity. The District Court, however, struck down the "indecent speech" provision of [the Dial-A-Porn Amendment], holding that in this respect the statute was overbroad and unconstitutional and that the result was consistent with *FCC v. Pacifica Foundation*. "While the government unquestionably has a legitimate interest in, e.g., protecting children from exposure to indecent dial-a-porn messages, [the Dial-A-Porn Amendment] is not narrowly drawn to achieve any such purpose. Its flat-out ban of indecent speech is contrary to the First Amendment." Therefore, the Court issued a preliminary injunction prohibiting enforcement of [the Dial-A-Porn Amendment] with respect to any communication alleged to be "indecent."

We [agreed to hear the case]. . . .

While dial-a-porn services are a creature of this decade, the medium, in its brief history, has been the subject of much litigation and the object of a series of attempts at regulation. The first litigation involving dial-a-porn was brought under [a federal statute] which proscribed [prohibited] knowingly "permitting a telephone under [one's] control" to be used to make "any comment, request, suggestion or proposal which is obscene, lewd, lascivious, filthy, or indecent." However, the FCC concluded in [a 1983] administrative action that the existing law did not cover dial-a-porn.

In reaction to that FCC determination, Congress made its first effort explicitly to address "dial-a-porn" when it added a subsection . . . to the 1934 Communications Act. The provision, which was the predecessor to the amendment at issue in this case, pertained directly to sexually-oriented commercial telephone messages and sought to restrict the access of minors to dial-a-porn. The relevant provision of the . . . Federal Communications Commission Authorization Act of 1983 made it a crime to use telephone facilities to make "obscene or indecent" interstate telephone communications "for commercial purposes to any person under eighteen years of age or to any other person without that person's consent." The statute criminalized commercial transmission of sexually-oriented communications to minors and required the FCC to promulgate regulations laying out the means by which dial-a-porn sponsors could screen out under-aged callers. The enactment provided that it would be a defense to prosecution that the defendant restricted access to adults only, in accordance with procedures established by the FCC. The statute did not criminalize sexually-oriented messages to adults, whether the messages were obscene or indecent.

The FCC initially promulgated regulations that would have established a defense to message providers operating only between the hours of 9 p.m. and 8 a.m. Eastern Time (time channeling) and to providers requiring payment by credit card (screening) before transmission of the dial-a-porn message. In *Carlin Communications, Inc. v. FCC* (1984), the Court of Appeals for the Second Circuit set aside the time channeling regulations and remanded [returned] to the FCC to examine other alternatives, concluding that the operating hours requirement was "both over-inclusive and under-inclusive" because it denied "access to adults between certain hours, but not to youths who can easily pick up a private or public telephone and call dial-a-porn during the remaining hours." The Court of Appeals did not reach [address] the constitutionality of the underlying legislation.

In 1985, the FCC promulgated new regulations which continued to permit credit card payment as a defense to prosecution. Instead of time restrictions, however, the Commission added a defense based on use of access codes (user identification codes). Thus, it would be a defense to prosecution under [the Dial-A-Porn Amendment] if the defendant, before transmission of the message, restricted customer access by requiring either payment by credit card or authorization by access or identification code. The regulations required each dial-a-porn vendor to develop an identification code data base and implementation scheme. Callers would be required to provide an access number for identification (or a credit card) before receiving the message. The access code would be received through the mail after the message provider reviewed the application and concluded through a written age ascertainment procedure that the applicant was at least eighteen years of age. The FCC rejected a proposal for "exchange blocking" which would block or screen telephone numbers at the customer's premises or at the telephone company offices. In *Carlin Communications, Inc. v. FCC* (1986), the Court of Appeals set aside the new regulations because of the FCC's failure adequately to consider customer premises blocking. Again, the constitutionality of the underlying legislation was not addressed.

The FCC then promulgated a third set of regulations, which again rejected customer premises blocking but added to the prior defenses of credit card payment and access code use a third defense - message scrambling. Under this system, providers would scramble the message, which would then be unintelligible without the use of a descrambler, the sale of which would be limited to adults. On January 15, 1988, in *Carlin Communications v. FCC*, the Court of Appeals for the Second Circuit held that the new regulations, which made access codes, along with credit card payments and scrambled messages, defenses to prosecution under [the Dial-A-Porn Amendment] for dial-a-porn providers, were supported by the evidence, had been properly arrived at, and were a "feasible and effective way to serve" the "compelling state interest" in protecting minors; but the Court directed the FCC to reopen proceedings if a less restrictive technology became available. The Court of Appeals, however, this time [addressing] the constitutionality of the statute, invalidated [the Dial-A-Porn Amendment] insofar as it sought to apply to nonobscene speech.

Thereafter, in April 1988, Congress [changed] [the Dial-A-Porn Amendment] of the Communications Act to prohibit indecent as well as obscene interstate commercial telephone communications directed to any person regardless of age. The amended statute, which took effect on July 1, 1988, also eliminated the requirement that the FCC promulgate regulations for restricting access to minors since a total ban was imposed on dial-a-porn, making it illegal for adults, as well as children, to have access to the sexually-explicit messages. It was this version of the statute that was in effect when Sable commenced this action.

In the ruling at issue in [the *Sable* appeal], the District Court upheld [the Dial-A-Porn Amendment]'s prohibition of obscene telephone messages as constitutional. We agree with that judgment. In contrast to the prohibition on indecent communications, there is no constitutional barrier to the ban on obscene dial-a-porn recordings. We have repeatedly held that the protection of the First Amendment does not extend to obscene speech. The cases before us today do not require us to decide what is obscene or what is indecent but rather to determine whether Congress is empowered to prohibit transmission of obscene telephonic communications.

. . . Sable argues that the legislation creates an impermissible national standard of obscenity, and that it places message senders in a "double bind" by compelling them to tailor all their messages to the least tolerant community. We do not read [the Dial-A-Porn Amendment] as contravening [violating] the "contemporary community standards" requirement of *Miller v. California.* [The Dial-A-Porn Amendment] no more establishes a "national standard" of obscenity than do federal statutes prohibiting the mailing of obscene materials, or the broadcasting of obscene messages. In *United States v. Reidel,* we said that Congress could prohibit the use of the mails for commercial distribution of materials properly classifiable as obscene, even though those materials were being distributed to willing adults who stated that they were adults. Similarly, we hold today that there is no constitutional stricture against Congress' prohibiting the interstate transmission of obscene commercial telephone recordings.

We stated in *United States v. 12 200-ft. Reels of Film* that the *Miller* standards, including the "contemporary community standards" formulation, apply to federal legislation. As we have said before, the fact that "distributors of allegedly obscene materials may be subjected to varying community standards in the various federal judicial districts into which they transmit the materials does not render a federal statute unconstitutional because of the failure of application of uniform national standards of obscenity."

Furthermore, Sable is free to tailor its messages, on a selective basis, if it so chooses, to the communities it chooses to serve. While Sable may be forced to incur some costs in developing and implementing a system for screening the locale of incoming calls, there is no constitutional impediment to enacting a law which may impose such costs on a medium electing to provide these messages. Whether Sable chooses to hire operators to determine the source of the calls or engages with the telephone company to arrange for the screening and blocking of out-of-area calls or finds another means for providing messages compatible with community standards is a decision for the message provider to make. There is no constitutional barrier under *Miller* to prohibiting communications that are obscene in some communities under local standards even though they are not obscene in others. If Sable's audience is comprised of different communities with different local standards, Sable ultimately bears the burden of complying with the prohibition on obscene messages.

In [the FCC appeal], the District Court concluded that while the Government has a legitimate interest in protecting children from exposure to indecent dial-a-porn messages, [the Dial-A-Porn Amendment] was not sufficiently narrowly drawn to serve that purpose and thus violated the First Amendment. We agree.

Sexual expression which is indecent but not obscene is protected by the First Amendment; and the federal parties do not submit that the sale of such materials to adults could be criminalized solely because they are indecent. The Government may, however, regulate the content of constitutionally protected speech in order to promote a compelling interest if it chooses the least restrictive means to further the articulated interest. We have recognized that there is a compelling interest in protecting the physical and psychological well-being of minors. This interest extends to shielding minors from the influence of literature that is not obscene by adult standards. The Government may serve this legitimate interest, but to withstand constitutional scrutiny, "it must do so by narrowly drawn regulations designed to serve those interests without unnecessarily interfering with First Amendment freedoms." It is not enough to show that the Government's ends are compelling; the means must be carefully tailored to achieve those ends.

In *Butler v. Michigan*, a unanimous Court reversed a conviction under a statute which made it an offense to make available to the general public materials found to have a potentially harmful influence on minors. The Court found the law to be insufficiently tailored since it denied adults their free speech rights by allowing them to read only what was acceptable for children. As Justice Frankfurter said in that case, "Surely this is to burn the house to roast the pig." In our judgment, this case, like *Butler*, presents us with "legislation not reasonably restricted to the evil with which it is said to deal."

In attempting to justify the complete ban and criminalization of the indecent commercial telephone communications with adults as well as minors, the federal parties rely on *FCC v. Pacifica*, a case in which the Court considered whether the FCC has the power to regulate a radio broadcast that is indecent but not obscene. In an emphatically narrow holding, the *Pacifica* Court concluded that special treatment of indecent broadcasting was justified.

Pacifica . . . did not involve a total ban on broadcasting indecent material. The FCC rule was not "'intended to place an absolute prohibition on the broadcast of this type of language, but rather sought to channel it to times of day when children most likely would not be exposed to it.'" The issue of a total ban was not before the Court.

The *Pacifica* opinion also relied on the "unique" attributes of broadcasting, noting that broadcasting is "uniquely pervasive," can intrude on the privacy of the home without prior warning as to program content, and is "uniquely accessible to children, even those too young to read." The private commercial telephone communications at issue here are substantially different from the public radio broadcast at issue in *Pacifica*. In contrast to public displays, unsolicited mailings and other means of expression which the recipient has no meaningful opportunity to avoid, the dial-it medium requires the listener to take affirmative steps to receive the communication. There is no "captive audience" problem here; callers will generally not be unwilling listeners. The context of dial-in services, where a caller seeks and is willing to pay for the communication, is manifestly different from a situation in which a listener does not want the received message. Placing a telephone call is not the same as turning on a radio and being taken by surprise by an indecent message. Unlike an unexpected outburst on a radio broadcast, the message received by one who places a call to a dial-a-porn service is not so invasive or surprising that it prevents an unwilling listener from avoiding exposure to it.

The Court in *Pacifica* was careful "to emphasize the narrowness of [its] holding." As we did in *Bolger v. Youngs Drug Products*, we . . . reiterate that "the government may not 'reduce the adult population to . . . only what is fit for children.'"

The federal parties nevertheless argue that the total ban on indecent commercial telephone communications is justified because nothing less could prevent children from gaining access to such messages. We find the argument quite unpersuasive. The FCC, after lengthy proceedings, determined that its credit card, access code, and scrambling rules were a satisfactory solution to the problem of keeping indecent dial-a-porn messages out of the reach of minors. The Court of Appeals, after careful consideration, agreed that these rules represented a "feasible and effective" way to serve the Government's compelling interest in protecting children.

The federal parties now insist that the rules would not be effective enough - that enterprising youngsters could and would evade the rules and gain access to communications from which they should be shielded. There is no evidence in the record before us to that effect, nor could there be since the FCC's implementation of [the Dial-A-Porn Amendment] prior to its 1988 amendment has never been tested over time. In this respect, the federal parties assert that in [changing the Dial-A-Porn Amendment] in 1988, Congress expressed its view that there was not a sufficiently effective way to protect minors short of the total ban that it enacted. The federal parties claim that we must give deference to that judgment.

To the extent that the federal parties suggest that we should defer to Congress' conclusion about an issue of constitutional law, our answer is that while we do not ignore it, it is our task in the end to decide whether Congress has violated the Constitution. This is particularly true where the Legislature has concluded that its product does not violate the First Amendment. "Deference to a legislative finding cannot limit judicial inquiry when First Amendment rights are at stake." The federal parties, however, also urge us to defer to the factual findings by Congress relevant to resolving the constitutional issue. . . . Beyond the fact that whatever deference is due legislative findings would not foreclose our independent judgment of the facts bearing on an issue of constitutional law, our answer is that the congressional record contains no legislative findings that would justify us in concluding that there is no constitutionally acceptable less restrictive means, short of a total ban, to achieve the Government's interest in protecting minors.

There is no doubt Congress enacted a total ban on both obscene and indecent telephone communications. But aside from conclusory statements during the debates by proponents of the bill, as well as similar assertions in hearings on a substantially identical bill the year before that under the FCC regulations minors could still have access to dial-a-porn messages, the congressional record presented to us contains no evidence as to how effective or ineffective the FCC's most recent regulations were or might prove to be. It may well be that there is no fail-safe method of guaranteeing that never will a minor be able to access the dial-a-porn system. The bill that was enacted, however, was introduced on the floor; nor was there a committee report on the bill from which the language of the enacted bill was taken. No Congressman or Senator purported to present a considered judgment with respect to how often or to what extent minors could or would circumvent the rules and have access to dial-a-porn messages. On the other hand, in the hearings on [the bill] the Committee heard testimony from the FCC and other witnesses that the FCC rules would be effective and should be tried out in practice. Furthermore, at the conclusion of the hearing, the Chairman of the Subcommittee suggested consultation looking toward "drafting a piece of legislation that will pass constitutional muster, while at the same time providing for the practical relief which families and groups are looking for." The bill never emerged from Committee.

For all we know from this record, the FCC's technological approach to restricting dial-a-porn messages to adults who seek them would be extremely effective, and only a few of the most enterprising and disobedient young people would manage to secure access to such messages. If this is the case, it seems to us that [the Dial-A-Porn Amendment] is not a narrowly tailored effort to serve the compelling interest of preventing minors from being exposed to indecent telephone messages. Under our precedents, [the Dial-A-Porn Amendment], in its present form, has the invalid effect of limiting the content of adult telephone conversations to that which is suitable for children to hear. It is another case of "burn[ing] up the house to roast the pig."

Because the statute's denial of adult access to telephone messages which are indecent but not obscene far exceeds that which is necessary to limit the access of minors to such messages, we hold that the ban does not survive constitutional scrutiny.

Accordingly, we affirm the judgment of the District Court in [both appeals].

"Filthy" School Library Books
Island Trees Schools v. Pico

We have found that these books contain material that is offensive to Christians and Jews, in particular, and Americans, in general. In addition these books contain obscenities, blasphemies, brutality, and perversion beyond description.

- The Island Trees School Board (1976)

On February 24, 1976 members of Long Island, New York's Island Trees School Board removed and banned from their junior and senior high school libraries books that its members believed to be "anti-American, anti-Christian, vulgar, immoral, and just plain filthy." The School Board stated, *It is our duty, our moral obligation, to protect the children in our schools from this moral danger as surely as from physical and medical dangers.*

The books banned from the high school were Vonnegut's *Slaughterhouse Five*, Morris' *The Naked Ape*, Thomas' *Down These Mean Streets*, Wright's *Black Boy*, Cleaver's *Soul On Ice*, LaFarge's *Laughing Boy*, Childress' *A Hero Ain't Nothin' But A Sandwich*, *The Best Short Stories Of Negro Writers* (an anthology edited by Langston Hughes), Malamud's *The Fixer*, and the anonymously-written *Go Ask Alice*.

On January 29, 1977 Steven Pico, an Island Trees student, along with other students, brought suit in United States District Court, claiming the Board had violated their First Amendment right to read, and demanding that the Board return the banned books to the library. On August 2, 1979 the District Court found in favor of the School Board. Pico appealed for a reversal. On March 3, 1981 the United States Court of Appeals found in favor of Pico. The School Board appealed for a reversal to the United States Supreme Court.

On June 25, 1982 the 5-4 decision of the Court was announced by Associate Justice William Brennan.

The *"Filthy" School Library Books* Court

Chief Justice Warren Burger
Appointed Chief Justice by President Nixon
Served 1969 - 1986

Associate Justice William Brennan
Appointed by President Eisenhower
Served 1956 - 1990

Associate Justice Byron White
Appointed by President Kennedy
Served 1962 - 1993

Associate Justice Thurgood Marshall
Appointed by President Lyndon Johnson
Served 1967 - 1991

Associate Justice Harry Blackmun
Appointed by President Nixon
Served 1970 - 1994

Associate Justice Lewis Powell
Appointed by President Nixon
Served 1971 - 1987

Associate Justice William Rehnquist
Appointed by President Nixon
Served 1971 -

Associate Justice John Paul Stevens
Appointed by President Ford
Served 1975 -

Associate Justice Sandra Day O'Connor
Appointed by President Reagan
Served 1981 -

The unedited text of *Island Trees. v. Pico* can be found in volume 457 of *United States Reports*. Our edited plain-English text follows.

ISLAND TREES SCHOOLS v. PICO
June 25, 1982

JUSTICE WILLIAM BRENNAN: The principal question presented is whether the First Amendment imposes limitations upon the exercise by a local school board of its discretion to remove library books from high school and junior high school libraries.

Petitioners are the Board of Education of the Island Trees Union Free School District No. 26, in New York, and . . . [Richard Ahrens,] the President of the Board, . . . [Frank Martin,] the Vice President, and . . . [other] Board members. The Board is a state agency charged with responsibility for the operation and administration of the public schools within the Island Trees School District. . . . Respondents are Steven Pico, Jacqueline Gold, Glenn Yarris, Russell Rieger, and Paul Sochinski . . . , students at the High School, and . . . Junior High School.

In September 1975, petitioners Ahrens, Martin, and [other School Board members] attended a conference sponsored by Parents of New York United (PONYU), a politically conservative organization of parents concerned about education legislation in the State of New York. At the conference these petitioners obtained lists of books described by Ahrens as "objectionable," and by Martin as "improper fare for school students." It was later determined that the High School library contained nine of the listed books [*Slaughter House Five, The Naked Ape, Down These Mean Streets, Best Short Stories of Negro Writers, Go Ask Alice, Laughing Boy, Black Boy, A Hero Ain't Nothin' But a Sandwich, and Soul on Ice*], and that another listed book [*A Reader for Writers*] was in the Junior High School library. In February 1976, at a meeting with the Superintendent of Schools and the Principals of the High School and Junior High School, the Board gave an "unofficial direction" that the listed books be removed from the library shelves and delivered to the Board's offices, so that Board members could read them. When this directive was carried out, it became publicized, and the Board issued a press release justifying its action. It characterized the removed books as "anti-American, anti-Christian, anti-Semitic, and just plain filthy," and concluded that "[i]t is our duty, our moral obligation, to protect the children in our schools from this moral danger as surely as from physical and medical dangers."

A short time later, the Board appointed a "Book Review Committee," consisting of four Island Trees parents and four members of the Island Trees schools staff, to read the listed books and to recommend to the Board whether the books should be retained, taking into account the books' "educational suitability," "good taste," "relevance," and "appropriateness to age and grade level." In July, the Committee made its final report to the Board, recommending that five of the listed books be retained and that two others be removed from the school libraries. As for the remaining four books, the Committee could not agree on two, took no position on one, and recommended that the last book be made available to students only with parental approval. The Board substantially rejected the Committee's report later that month, deciding that only one book should be returned to the High School library without restriction, that another should be made available subject to parental approval, but that the remaining nine books should "be removed from elementary and secondary libraries and [from] use in the curriculum." The Board gave no reasons for rejecting the recommendations of the Committee that it had appointed.

[The students] reacted to the Board's decision by bringing the present action. They alleged that [the Board] had "ordered the removal of the books from school libraries and proscribed [prohibited] their use in the curriculum because particular passages in the books offended their social, political, and moral tastes and not because the books, taken as a whole, were lacking in educational value."

[Pico and his fellow students] claimed that the Board's actions denied them their rights under the First Amendment. They asked the court for a declaration that the Board's actions were unconstitutional, and for [the court to order] the Board to return the nine books to the school libraries and to refrain from interfering with the use of those books in the schools' curricula.

The District Court granted summary [immediate] judgment in favor of [the School Board]. In the court's view, "the parties substantially agree[d] about the motivation behind the board's actions," - namely, that

"the board acted not on religious principles but on its conservative educational philosophy, and on its belief that the nine books removed from the school library and curriculum were irrelevant, vulgar, immoral, and in bad taste, making them educationally unsuitable for the district's junior and senior high school students."

With this factual premise as its background, the court rejected [the students'] contention that their First Amendment rights had been infringed by the Board's actions. Noting that statutes, history, and precedent [prior cases] had vested local school boards with a broad discretion to formulate educational policy, the court concluded that it should not intervene in "'the daily operations of school systems'" unless "'basic constitutional values'" were "'sharply implicate[d]',"and determined that the conditions for such intervention did not exist in the present case. Acknowledging that the "removal [of the books] . . . clearly was content-based," the court nevertheless found no constitutional violation of the requisite magnitude,

> "The board has restricted access only to certain books which the board believed to be, in essence, vulgar. While removal of such books from a school library may . . . reflect a misguided educational philosophy, it does not constitute a sharp and direct infringement of any First Amendment right."

A three-judge panel of the United States Court of Appeals . . . reversed the judgment of the District Court. . . . Judge Newman . . . viewed the case as turning on the contested factual issue of whether [the School Board's] removal decision was motivated by a justifiable desire to remove books containing vulgarities and sexual explicitness, or rather by an impermissible desire to suppress ideas.

. . . . Our precedents have long recognized certain constitutional limits upon the power of the State to control even the curriculum and classroom. For example, *Meyer v. Nebraska* struck down a state law that forbade the teaching of modern foreign languages in public and private schools, and *Epperson v. Arkansas* declared unconstitutional a state law that prohibited the teaching of the Darwinian theory of evolution in any state-supported school. But the current action does not require us to re-enter this difficult terrain, which *Meyer* and *Epperson* traversed without apparent misgiving. For as this case is presented to us, it does not involve textbooks, or indeed any books that Island Trees students would be required to read. [The students] do not seek in this Court to impose limitations upon their School Board's discretion to prescribe the curricula of the Island Trees schools. On the contrary, the only books at issue in this case are library books, books that by their nature are optional rather than required reading. Our adjudication of the present case thus does not intrude into the classroom, or into the compulsory courses taught there. Furthermore, even as to library books, the action before us does not involve the acquisition of books. [The students] have not sought to compel their School Board to add to the school library shelves any books that students desire to read. Rather, the only action challenged in this case is the *removal* from school libraries of books originally placed there by the school authorities, or without objection from them.

. . . . [T]he issue before us . . . is a narrow one. . . . [D]oes the First Amendment impose *any* limitations upon the discretion of [the School Board] to remove library books from the Island Trees High School and Junior High School? . . .

The Court has long recognized that local school boards have broad discretion in the management of school affairs. *Epperson* . . . reaffirmed that, by and large, "public education in our Nation is committed to the control of state and local authorities," and that federal courts should not ordinarily "intervene in the resolution of conflicts which arise in the daily operation of school systems." *Tinker v. Des Moines School District* noted that we have "repeatedly emphasized . . . the comprehensive authority of the States and of school officials . . . to prescribe and control conduct in the schools." We have also acknowledged that public schools are vitally important "in the preparation of individuals for participation as citizens," and as vehicles for "inculcating fundamental values necessary to the maintenance of a democratic political system." We are therefore in full agreement with [the School Board] that local school boards must be permitted "to establish and apply their curriculum in such a way as to transmit community values," and that "there is a legitimate and substantial community interest in promoting respect for authority and traditional values be they social, moral, or political."

At the same time, however, we have necessarily recognized that the discretion of the States and local school boards in matters of education must be exercised in a manner that comports with the transcendent imperatives of the First Amendment. In *West Virginia Board of Education v. Barnette*, we held that under the First Amendment a student in a public school could not be compelled to salute the flag. We reasoned,

> "Boards of Education . . . have, of course, important, delicate, and highly discretionary functions, but none that they may not perform within the limits of the Bill of Rights. That they are educating the young for citizenship is reason for scrupulous protection of Constitutional freedoms of the individual, if we are not to strangle the free mind at its source and teach youth to discount important principles of our government as mere platitudes."

Later cases have consistently followed this rationale. Thus *Epperson* . . . invalidated a State's anti-evolution statute as violative of the Establishment Clause, and reaffirmed the duty of federal courts "to apply the First Amendment's mandate in our educational system where essential to safeguard the fundamental values of freedom of speech and inquiry." And *Tinker* . . . held that a local school board had infringed the free speech rights of high school and junior high school students by suspending them from school for wearing black armbands in class as a protest against the Government's policy in Vietnam; we stated there that the "comprehensive authority . . . of school officials" must be exercised "consistent with fundamental constitutional safeguards." In sum, students do not "shed their constitutional rights to freedom of speech or expression at the schoolhouse gate," and therefore local school boards must discharge their "important, delicate, and highly discretionary functions" within the limits and constraints of the First Amendment.

The nature of students' First Amendment rights in the context of this case requires further examination. . . . *Barnette* is instructive. There the Court held that students' liberty of conscience could not be infringed in the name of "national unity" or "patriotism." We explained that

> "the action of the local authorities in compelling the flag salute and pledge transcends constitutional limitations on their power and invades the sphere of intellect and spirit which it is the purpose of the First Amendment to our Constitution to reserve from all official control."

Similarly, *Tinker* . . . held that students' rights to freedom of expression of their political views could not be abridged by reliance upon an "undifferentiated fear or apprehension of disturbance" arising from such expression,

> "Any departure from absolute regimentation may cause trouble. Any variation from the majority's opinion may inspire fear. Any word spoken, in class, in the lunch-room, or on the campus, that deviates from the views of another person may start an argument or cause a disturbance. But our Constitution says we must take this risk; and our history says that it is this sort of hazardous free-dom - this kind of openness - that is the basis of our na-tional strength and of the independence and vigor of Americans who grow up and live in this . . . often dis-putatious society."

In short, "First Amendment rights, applied in light of the special characteristics of the school environment, are avail-able to . . . students."

Of course, courts should not "intervene in the resolution of conflicts which arise in the daily operation of school systems" unless "basic constitutional values" are "directly and sharply implicate[d]" in those conflicts. But we think that the First Amendment rights of students may be directly and sharply implicated by the removal of books from the shelves of a school library. Our precedents have focused "not only on the role of the First Amendment in fostering individual self-expression but also on its role in affording the public access to discussion, debate, and the dissemination of information and ideas." And we have recognized that "the State may not, consistently with the spirit of the First Amendment, contract the spectrum of available knowledge." In keeping with this principle, we have held that in a variety of contexts "the Constitution protects the right to receive information and ideas." This right is an inherent corollary of the rights of free speech and press that are explicitly guaranteed by the Constitution, in two senses. First, the right to receive ideas follows ineluctably from the sender's First Amendment right to send them - "The right of freedom of speech and press . . . embraces the right to distribute literature, and necessarily protects the right to receive it." "The dissemination of ideas can accomplish nothing if otherwise willing addressees are not free to receive and consider them. It would be a barren marketplace of ideas that had only sellers and no buyers."

More importantly, the right to receive ideas is a necessary predicate to the recipient's meaningful exercise of his own rights of speech, press, and political freedom. Madison admonished us,

"A popular Government, without popular information, or the means of acquiring it, is but a Prologue to a Farce or a Tragedy, or perhaps both. Knowledge will forever govern ignorance. And a people who mean to be their own Governors, must arm themselves with the power which knowledge gives."

As we recognized in *Tinker*, students too are beneficiaries of this principle,

> "In our system, students may not be regarded as closed-circuit recipients of only that which the State chooses to communicate. . . . [S]chool officials cannot suppress 'expressions of feeling with which they do not wish to contend.'"

In sum, just as access to ideas makes it possible for citizens generally to exercise their rights of free speech and press in a meaningful manner, such access prepares students for active and effective participation in the pluralistic, often contentious society in which they will soon be adult members. Of course all First Amendment rights accorded to students must be construed [interpreted] "in light of the special characteristics of the school environment." But the special characteristics of the school library make that environment especially appropriate for the recognition of the First Amendment rights of students.

A school library, no less than any other public library, is "a place dedicated to quiet, to knowledge, and to beauty." *Keyishian v. Board of Regents* observed that "'students must always remain free to inquire, to study and to evaluate, to gain new maturity and understanding.'" The school library is the principal locus of such freedom. As one District Court has well put it, in the school library

> "a student can literally explore the unknown, and discover areas of interest and thought not covered by the prescribed curriculum. . . . Th[e] student learns that a library is a place to test or expand upon ideas presented to him, in or out of the classroom."

[The School Board] emphasize[s] the inculcative function of secondary education, and argue[s] that [it] must be allowed unfettered discretion to "transmit community values" through the Island Trees schools. But that sweeping claim overlooks the unique role of the school library. It appears from the record that use of the Island Trees school libraries is completely voluntary on the part of students. Their selection of books from these libraries is entirely a matter of free choice; the libraries afford them an opportunity at self-education and individual enrichment that is wholly optional. [The School Board] might well defend their claim of absolute discretion in matters of curriculum by reliance upon their duty to inculcate community values. But we think that [their] reliance upon that duty is misplaced where, as here, they attempt to extend their claim of absolute discretion beyond the compulsory environment of the classroom, into the school library and the regime of voluntary inquiry that there holds sway.

In rejecting [the School Board's] claim of absolute discretion to remove books from their school libraries, we do not deny that local school boards have a substantial legitimate role to play in the determination of school library content. We thus must turn to the question of the extent to which the First Amendment places limitations upon the discretion of [the School Board] to remove books from their libraries. In this inquiry we enjoy the guidance of several precedents. . . . *Barnette* stated,

"If there is any fixed star in our constitutional constellation, it is that no official, high or petty, can prescribe what shall be orthodox in politics, nationalism, religion, or other matters of opinion. . . . If there are any circumstances which permit an exception, they do not now occur to us."

This doctrine has been reaffirmed in later cases involving education. For example, *Keyishian* . . . noted that "the First Amendment . . . does not tolerate laws that cast a pall of orthodoxy over the classroom." . . .

With respect to the present case, the message of these precedents is clear. [The School Board] rightly possess[es] significant discretion to determine the content of their school libraries. But that discretion may not be exercised in a narrowly partisan or political manner. If a Democratic school board, motivated by party affiliation, ordered the removal of all books written by or in favor of Republicans, few would doubt that the order violated the constitutional rights of the students denied access to those books. The same conclusion would surely apply if an all-white school board, motivated by racial animus, decided to remove all books authored by blacks or advocating racial equality and integration. Our Constitution does not permit the official suppression of ideas. Thus whether [the School Board's] removal of books from their school libraries denied [the students] their First Amendment rights depends upon the motivation behind [the School Board's] actions. If [the School Board] intended by [its] removal decision to deny [the students] access to ideas with which [the School Board] disagreed, and if this intent was the decisive factor in [the School Board's] decision, then [the School Board has] exercised [its] discretion in violation of the Constitution. To permit such intentions to control official actions would be to encourage the precise sort of officially prescribed orthodoxy unequivocally condemned in *Barnette*. On the other hand, [the students] implicitly concede that an unconstitutional motivation would not be demonstrated if it were shown that [the School Board] had decided to remove the books at issue because those books were pervasively vulgar. And again, [the students] concede that if it were demonstrated that the removal decision was based solely upon the "educational suitability" of the books in question, then their removal would be "perfectly permissible." In other words, in [the students'] view such motivations, if decisive of [the School Board's] actions, would not carry the danger of an official suppression of ideas, and thus would not violate [the students'] First Amendment rights.

As noted earlier, nothing in our decision today affects in any way the discretion of a local school board to choose books to add to the libraries of their schools. Because we are concerned in this case with the suppression of ideas, our holding today affects only the discretion to remove books. In brief, we hold that local school boards may not remove books from school library shelves simply because they dislike the ideas contained in those books and seek by their removal to "prescribe what shall be orthodox in politics, nationalism, religion, or other matters of opinion." Such purposes stand inescapably condemned by our precedents. . . . Affirmed.

Child Pornography
New York v. Ferber

The care of children is a sacred trust and should not be abused by those who seek to profit through a commercial network based upon the exploitation of children. The public policy of the state demands the protection of children from exploitation through sexual performances.
- The New York State Legislature (1977)

In 1977 the New York State Legislature, in a effort to fight the pornography industry's sexual exploitation of children, enacted a Child Pornography Law. New York's Child Pornography Law criminalized the production and sale of any visual depiction, legally obscene or not, of children under sixteen years of age engaged in sexual conduct. Paul Ferber, the owner of a New York City adult bookstore, sold two films depicting young boys engaged in prohibited sexual conduct to police undercover agents, who arrested him under the State's Child Pornography Law.

Tried and convicted in New York County Court of selling the prohibited films, Ferber faced a maximum penalty of seven years imprisonment. He appealed (on First Amendment grounds) for a reversal of his conviction to the New York State Court of Appeals.

On May 12, 1981 the New York State Court of Appeals reversed the conviction, finding that the State's Child Pornography Law violated the First Amendment. New York appealed to the United States Supreme Court. The Court agreed to answer this question - *To prevent the abuse of children who are made to engage in sexual conduct for commercial purposes, can the New York State Legislature, consistent with the First Amendment, prohibit the dissemination of material which shows children engaged in sexual conduct, regardless of whether such material is obscene?*

On July 2, 1982 the 9-0 decision of the Court was announced by Associate Justice Byron White.

The *Child Pornography* Court

Chief Justice Warren Burger
Appointed Chief Justice by President Nixon
Served 1969 - 1986

Associate Justice William Brennan
Appointed by President Eisenhower
Served 1956 - 1990

Associate Justice Potter Stewart
Appointed by President Eisenhower
Served 1958 - 1981

Associate Justice Byron White
Appointed by President Kennedy
Served 1962 - 1993

Associate Justice Thurgood Marshall
Appointed by President Lyndon Johnson
Served 1967 - 1991

Associate Justice Harry Blackmun
Appointed by President Nixon
Served 1970 - 1994

Associate Justice Lewis Powell
Appointed by President Nixon
Served 1971 - 1987

Associate Justice William Rehnquist
Appointed by President Nixon
Served 1971 -

Associate Justice John Paul Stevens
Appointed by President Ford
Served 1975 -

The unedited text of *New York v. Ferber* can be found in volume 458 of *United States Reports*. Our edited plain-English text follows.

NEW YORK v. FERBER
July 2, 1982

JUSTICE BYRON WHITE: At issue in this case is the constitutionality of a New York criminal statute which prohibits persons from knowingly promoting sexual performances by children under the age of sixteen by distributing material which depicts such performances.

In recent years, the exploitive use of children in the production of pornography has become a serious national problem. The Federal Government and forty-seven States have sought to combat the problem with statutes specifically directed at the production of child pornography. At least half of such statutes do not require that the materials produced be legally obscene. Thirty-five States and the United States Congress have also passed legislation prohibiting the distribution of such materials; twenty States prohibit the distribution of material depicting children engaged in sexual conduct without requiring that the material be legally obscene.

New York is one of the twenty. In 1977, the New York Legislature enacted [the Child Pornography Law, which] criminalizes as a class C felony the use of a child in a sexual performance - "A person is guilty of the use of a child in a sexual performance if knowing the character and content thereof he employs, authorizes, or induces a child less than sixteen years of age to engage in a sexual performance or being a parent, legal guardian, or custodian of such child, he consents to the participation by such child in a sexual performance."

A "[s]exual performance" is defined as "any performance or part thereof which includes sexual conduct by a child less than sixteen years of age." "Sexual conduct" is in turn defined - "Sexual conduct" means actual or simulated sexual intercourse, deviate sexual intercourse, sexual bestiality, masturbation, sado-masochistic abuse, or lewd exhibition of the genitals." A performance is defined as "any play, motion picture, photograph or dance" or "any other visual representation exhibited before an audience."

At issue in this case is Section 263.15 [the performance section], defining a class D felony - "A person is guilty of promoting a sexual performance by a child when, knowing the character and content thereof, he produces, directs, or promotes any performance which includes sexual conduct by a child less than sixteen years of age."

To "promote" is also defined - "Promote" means to procure, manufacture, issue, sell, give, provide, lend, mail, deliver, transfer, transmute, publish, distribute, circulate, disseminate, present, exhibit or advertise, or to offer or agree to do the same."

A companion provision [Section 263.10] bans only the knowing dissemination of obscene material.

This case arose when Paul Ferber, the proprietor of a Manhattan bookstore specializing in sexually-oriented products, sold two films to an undercover police officer. The films are devoted almost exclusively to depicting young boys masturbating. Ferber was indicted [charged] on two counts of violating [the knowing dissemination section] and two counts of violating [the performance section], the two New York laws controlling dissemination of child pornography. After a jury trial, Ferber was acquitted [found innocent] of the two counts of promoting an obscene sexual performance, but found guilty of the two counts under [the performance section], which did not require proof that the films were obscene. Ferber's convictions were affirmed [upheld] by the Appellate Division of the New York State Supreme Court.

The New York Court of Appeals reversed, holding that [the performance section] violated the First Amendment. The court began by noting that, in light of [the knowing dissemination section]'s explicit inclusion of an obscenity standard, [the performance section] could not be construed [interpreted] to include such a standard. Therefore, "the statute would . . . prohibit the promotion of materials which are traditionally entitled to constitutional protection from government interference under the First Amendment." Although the court recognized the State's "legitimate interest in protecting the welfare of minors" and noted that this "interest may transcend First Amendment concerns," it nevertheless found two fatal defects in the New York statute. [The performance section] was underinclusive because it discriminated against visual portrayals of children engaged in sexual activity by not also prohibiting the distribution of films of other dangerous activity. It was also overbroad because it prohibited the distribution of materials produced outside the State, as well as materials, such as medical books and educational sources, which "deal with adolescent sex in a realistic but nonobscene manner." Two judges dissented. We granted the State's petition for certiorari [agreed to hear the case and consider] the single question - "To prevent the abuse of children who are made to engage in sexual conduct for commercial purposes, could the New York State Legislature, consistent with the First Amendment, prohibit the dissemination of material which shows children engaged in sexual conduct, regardless of whether such material is obscene?"

The Court of Appeals proceeded on the assumption that the standard of obscenity incorporated in [the knowing dissemination section], which follows the guidelines enunciated in *Miller v. California*, constitutes the appropriate line dividing protected from unprotected expression by which to measure a regulation directed at child pornography. It was on the premise that "nonobscene adolescent sex" could not be singled out for special treatment that the court found [the performance section] "strikingly underinclusive." . . .

The Court of Appeals' assumption was not unreasonable in light of our decisions. This case, however, constitutes our first examination of a statute directed at and limited to depictions of sexual activity involving children. We believe our inquiry should begin with the question of whether a State has somewhat more freedom in proscribing [prohibiting] works which portray sexual acts or lewd exhibitions of genitalia by children.

In *Chaplinsky v. New Hampshire*, the Court laid the foundation for the excision of obscenity from the realm of constitutionally protected expression,

> "There are certain well-defined and narrowly limited classes of speech, the prevention and punishment of which have never been thought to raise any Constitutional problem. These include the lewd and obscene. . . . It has been well observed that such utterances are no essential part of any exposition of ideas, and are of such slight social value as a step to truth that any benefit that may be derived from them is clearly outweighed by the social interest in order and morality."

Embracing this judgment, the Court squarely held in *Roth v. United States* that "obscenity is not within the area of constitutionally protected speech or press." The Court recognized that "rejection of obscenity as utterly without redeeming social importance" was implicit in the history of the First Amendment - the original States provided for the prosecution of libel, blasphemy, and profanity, and the "universal judgment that obscenity should be restrained [is] reflected in the international agreement of over fifty nations, in the obscenity laws of all of the forty-eight states, and in the twenty obscenity laws enacted by Congress from 1842 to 1956.

Roth was followed by fifteen years during which this Court struggled with "the intractable obscenity problem." Despite considerable vacillation over the proper definition of obscenity, a majority of the Members of the Court remained firm in the position that "the States have a legitimate interest in prohibiting dissemination or exhibition of obscene material when the mode of dissemination carries with it a significant danger of offending the sensibilities of unwilling recipients or of exposure to juveniles."

Throughout this period, we recognized "the inherent dangers of undertaking to regulate any form of expression." Consequently, our difficulty was not only to assure that statutes designed to regulate obscene materials sufficiently defined what was prohibited, but also to devise substantive limits on what fell within the permissible scope of regulation. In *Miller v. California*, a majority of the Court agreed that a "state offense must also be limited to works which, taken as a whole, appeal to the prurient interest in sex, which portray sexual conduct in a patently offensive way, and which, taken as a whole, do not have serious literary, artistic, political, or scientific value." Over the past decade, we have adhered to the guidelines expressed in *Miller*, which subsequently has been followed in the regulatory schemes of most States.

The *Miller* standard, like its predecessors, was an accommodation between the State's interests in protecting the "sensibilities of unwilling recipients" from exposure to pornographic material and the dangers of censorship inherent in unabashedly content-based laws. Like obscenity statutes, laws directed at the dissemination of child pornography run the risk of suppressing protected expression by allowing the hand of the censor to become unduly heavy. For the following reasons, however, we are persuaded that the States are entitled to greater leeway in the regulation of porno-graphic depictions of children.

First. It is evident beyond the need for elaboration that a State's interest in "safeguarding the physical and psychological well-being of a minor" is "compelling." "A democratic society rests, for its continuance, upon the healthy, well-rounded growth of young people into full maturity as citizens." Accordingly, we have sustained [upheld] legislation aimed at protecting the physical and emotional well-being of youth, even when the laws have operated in the sensitive area of constitutionally protected rights. In *Prince v. Massachusetts*, the Court held that a statute prohibiting use of a child to distribute literature on the street was valid notwithstanding the statute's effect on a First Amendment activity. In *Ginsberg v. New York*, we sustained a New York law protecting children from exposure to nonobscene literature. Most recently, we held that the Government's interest in the "well-being of its youth" justified special treatment of inde-cent broadcasting received by adults as well as children.

The prevention of sexual exploitation and abuse of children constitutes a government objective of surpassing impor-tance. The legislative findings accompanying passage of the New York laws reflect this concern,

> "[T]here has been a proliferation of exploitation of chil-dren as subjects in sexual performances. The care of children is a sacred trust and should not be abused by those who seek to profit through a commercial network based upon the exploitation of children. The public policy of the state demands the protection of children from exploitation through sexual performances."

We shall not second-guess this legislative judgment. . . . [V]irtually all of the States and the United States have passed legislation proscribing the production of or otherwise combating "child pornography." The legislative judgment, as well as the judgment found in the relevant literature, is that the use of children as subjects of pornographic materials is harmful to the physiological, emotional, and mental health of the child. That judgment, we think, easily passes muster under the First Amendment.

Second. The distribution of photographs and films depicting sexual activity by juveniles is intrinsically related to the sexual abuse of children in at least two ways. First, the materials produced are a permanent record of the children's participation and the harm to the child is exacerbated by their circulation. Second, the distribution network for child pornography must be closed if the production of material which requires the sexual exploitation of children is to be effectively controlled. Indeed, there is no serious contention that the legislature was unjustified in believing that it is difficult, if not impossible, to halt the exploitation of children by pursuing only those who produce the photographs and movies. While the production of pornographic materials is a low profile, clandestine industry, the need to market the resulting products requires a visible apparatus of distribution. The most expeditious, if not the only practical, method of law enforcement may be to dry up the market for this material by imposing severe criminal penalties on persons selling, advertising, or otherwise promoting the product. Thirty-five States and Congress have concluded that restraints on the distribution of pornographic materials are required in order to effectively combat the problem, and there is a body of literature and testimony to support these legislative conclusions.

[Ferber] does not contend that the State is unjustified in pursuing those who distribute child pornography. Rather, he argues that it is enough for the State to prohibit the distribution of materials that are legally obscene under the *Miller* test. While some States may find that this approach properly accommodates its interests, it does not follow that the First Amendment prohibits a State from going further. The *Miller* standard, like all general definitions of what may be banned as obscene, does not reflect the State's particular and more compelling interest in prosecuting those who promote the sexual exploitation of children. Thus, the question under the *Miller* test of whether a work, taken as a whole, appeals to the prurient interest of the average person bears no connection to the issue of whether a child has been physically or psychologically harmed in the production of the work. Similarly, a sexually explicit depiction need not be "patently offensive" in order to have required the sexual exploitation of a child for its production. In addition, a work which, taken on the whole, contains serious literary, artistic, political, or scientific value may nevertheless embody the hardest core of child pornography. "It is irrelevant to the child [who has been abused] whether or not the material . . . has a literary, artistic, political or social value." We therefore cannot conclude that the *Miller* standard is a satisfactory solution to the child pornography problem.

Third. The advertising and selling of child pornography provide an economic motive for, and are thus an integral part of, the production of such materials, an activity illegal throughout the Nation. "It rarely has been suggested that the constitutional freedom for speech and press extends its immunity to speech or writing used as an integral part of conduct in violation of a valid criminal statute." We note that, were the statutes outlawing the employment of children in these films and photographs fully effective (and the constitutionality of these laws has not been questioned), the First Amendment implications would be no greater than that presented by laws against distribution - enforceable production laws would leave no child pornography to be marketed.

Fourth. The value of permitting live performances and photographic reproductions of children engaged in lewd sexual conduct is exceedingly modest. . . . We consider it unlikely that visual depictions of children performing sexual acts or lewdly exhibiting their genitals would often constitute an important and necessary part of a literary performance or scientific or educational work. As a state judge in this case observed, if it were necessary for literary or artistic value, a person over the statutory age who perhaps looked younger could be utilized. Simulation outside of the prohibition of the statute could provide another alternative. Nor is there any question here of censoring a particular literary theme or portrayal of sexual activity. The First Amendment interest is limited to that of rendering the portrayal somewhat more "realistic" by utilizing or photographing children.

Fifth. Recognizing and classifying child pornography as a category of material outside the protection of the First Amendment is not incompatible with our earlier decisions. "The question whether speech is, or is not, protected by the First Amendment often depends on the content of the speech." . . . When a definable class of material, such as that covered by [the performance section], bears so heavily and pervasively on the welfare of children engaged in its production, we think the balance of competing interests is clearly struck, and that it is permissible to consider these materials as without the protection of the First Amendment.

There are, of course, limits on the category of child pornography which, like obscenity, is unprotected by the First Amendment. As with all legislation in this sensitive area, the conduct to be prohibited must be adequately defined by the applicable state law, as written or authoritatively construed. Here the nature of the harm to be combated requires that the state offense be limited to works that visually depict sexual conduct by children below a specified age. The category of "sexual conduct" proscribed must also be suitably limited and described.

The test for child pornography is separate from the obscenity standard enunciated in *Miller*, but may be compared to it for the purpose of clarity. The *Miller* formulation is adjusted in the following respects - a trier of fact [judge or jury] need not find that the material appeals to the prurient interest of the average person; it is not required that sexual conduct portrayed be done so in a patently offensive manner; and the material at issue need not be considered as a whole. We note that the distribution of descriptions or other depictions of sexual conduct, not otherwise obscene, which do not involve live performance or photographic or other visual reproduction of live performances, retains First Amendment protection. As with obscenity laws, criminal responsibility may not be imposed without some element of scienter [guilty knowledge] on the part of the defendant [the accused].

[The performance section]'s prohibition incorporates a definition of sexual conduct that comports with the above-stated principles. The forbidden acts to be depicted are listed with sufficient precision and represent the kind of conduct that, if it were the theme of a work, could render it legally obscene - "actual or simulated sexual intercourse, deviate sexual intercourse, sexual bestiality, masturbation, sado-masochistic abuse, or lewd exhibition of the genitals." The term "lewd exhibition of the genitals" is not unknown in this area and, indeed, was given in *Miller* as an example of a permissible regulation. A performance is defined only to include live or visual depictions - "any play, motion picture, photograph or dance . . . [or] other visual representation exhibited before an audience." [The performance section] expressly includes a [guilty knowledge] requirement.

We hold that [the performance section] sufficiently describes a category of material the production and distribution of which is not entitled to First Amendment protection. It is therefore clear that there is nothing unconstitutionally "underinclusive" about a statute that singles out this category of material for proscription. It also follows that the State is not barred by the First Amendment from prohibiting the distribution of unprotected materials produced outside the State.

It remains to address the claim that the New York statute is unconstitutionally overbroad because it would forbid the distribution of material with serious literary, scientific, or educational value or material which does not threaten the harms sought to be combated by the State. [Ferber] prevailed on that ground [in the lower court], and it is to that issue that we now turn.

The New York Court of Appeals . . . [found] that [the performance section] was fatally overbroad:

> "[T]he statute would prohibit the showing of any play or movie in which a child portrays a defined sexual act, real or simulated, in a nonobscene manner. It would also prohibit the sale, showing, or distributing of medical or educational materials containing photographs of such acts. Indeed, by its terms, the statute would prohibit those who oppose such portrayals from providing illustrations of what they oppose."

While the construction that a state court gives a state statute is not a matter subject to our review, this Court is the final arbiter of whether the Federal Constitution necessitated the invalidation of a state law. It is only through this process of review that we may correct erroneous applications of the Constitution that err on the side of an overly broad reading of our doctrines and precedents [prior cases], as well as state court decisions giving the Constitution too little shrift. . . .

The traditional rule is that a person to whom a statute may constitutionally be applied may not challenge that statute on the ground that it may conceivably be applied unconstitutionally to others in situations not before the Court. By focusing on the factual situation before us, and similar cases necessary for development of a constitutional rule, we face "flesh-and-blood" legal problems with data "relevant and adequate to an informed judgment." This practice also fulfills a valuable institutional purpose - it allows state courts the opportunity to construe a law to avoid constitutional infirmities.

What has come to be known as the First Amendment overbreadth doctrine is one of the few exceptions to this principle, and must be justified by "weighty countervailing policies." The doctrine is predicated on the sensitive nature of protected expression - "persons whose expression is constitutionally protected may well refrain from exercising their rights for fear of criminal sanctions by a statute susceptible of application to protected expression." It is for this reason that we have allowed persons to attack overly broad statutes even though the conduct of the person making the attack is clearly unprotected, and could be proscribed by a law drawn with the requisite specificity.

The scope of the First Amendment overbreadth doctrine, like most exceptions to established principles, must be carefully tied to the circumstances in which . . . invalidation of a statute is truly warranted. Because of the wide-reaching effects of striking down a statute on its face at the request of one whose own conduct may be punished despite the First Amendment, we have recognized that the overbreadth doctrine is "strong medicine," and have employed it with hesitation, and then "only as a last resort." . . .

Broadrick v. Oklahoma examined a regulation involving restrictions on political campaign activity, an area not considered "pure speech," and thus it was unnecessary to consider the proper overbreadth test when a law arguably reaches traditional forms of expression such as books and films. As we intimated in *Broadrick*, the requirement of substantial overbreadth extended "at the very least" to cases involving conduct plus speech. This case, which poses the question squarely, convinces us that the rationale of *Broadrick* is sound, and should be applied in the present context involving the harmful employment of children to make sexually explicit materials for distribution.

. . . . While a sweeping statute, or one incapable of limitation, has the potential to repeatedly chill the exercise of expressive activity by many individuals, the extent of deterrence of protected speech can be expected to decrease with the declining reach of the regulation. This observation appears equally applicable to the publication of books and films as it is to activities, such as picketing or participation in election campaigns, which have previously been categorized as involving conduct plus speech. We see no appreciable difference between the position of a publisher or bookseller in doubt as to the reach of New York's child pornography law and the situation faced by the Oklahoma state employees with respect to that State's restriction on partisan political activity. Indeed, it could reasonably be argued that the bookseller, with an economic incentive to sell materials that may fall within the statute's scope, may be less likely to be deterred than the employee who wishes to engage in political campaign activity.

. . . . [W]e hold that [the performance section] is not substantially overbroad. We consider this the paradigmatic case of a state statute whose legitimate reach dwarfs its arguably impermissible applications. New York, as we have held, may constitutionally prohibit dissemination of material specified in [the performance section]. While the reach of the statute is directed at the hard core of child pornography, the Court of Appeals was understandably concerned that some protected expression, ranging from medical textbooks to pictorials in the National Geographic, would fall prey to the statute. How often, if ever, it may be necessary to employ children to engage in conduct clearly within the reach of [the performance section] in order to produce educational, medical, or artistic works cannot be known with certainty. Yet we seriously doubt, and it has not been suggested, that these arguably impermissible applications of the statute amount to more than a tiny fraction of the materials within the statute's reach. Nor will we assume that the New York courts will widen the possibly invalid reach of the statute by giving an expansive construction to the proscription on "lewd exhibition[s] of the genitals." Under these circumstances, [the performance section] is "not substantially overbroad, and . . . whatever overbreadth may exist should be cured through case-by-case analysis of the fact situations to which its sanctions, assertedly, may not be applied."

Because [the performance section] is not substantially overbroad, it is unnecessary to consider its application to material that does not depict sexual conduct of a type that New York may restrict consistent with the First Amendment. As applied to Paul Ferber and to others who distribute similar material, the statute does not violate the First Amendment as applied to the States through the Fourteenth. The decision of the New York Court of Appeals is reversed, and the case is remanded [returned] to that court for further proceedings not inconsistent with this opinion.

The Seven Words You Can't Say On The Radio
FCC v. Pacifica Foundation

Nothing in [the Federal Radio] Act shall be understood or construed to give the licensing authority the power of censorship over radio communications . . . and no regulation or condition shall be fixed by the licensing authority which shall interfere with the right of free speech on the radio. **- The Federal Radio Act of 1927**

On Tuesday, October 30, 1973, comedian George Carlin's live recording of *Filthy Words*, a twelve-minute satiric monologue on "the words you can't say on the public airwaves" was played on New York City radio station WBAI, owned by the Pacifica Foundation. Prior to the broadcast, which was made about 2 o'clock in the afternoon, listeners were warned that Carlin's *Filthy Words* "included sensitive language which might be regarded as offensive to some."

A complaint was made to the Federal Communications Commission (FCC) by a parent whose young son had heard the broadcast.

The FCC, to which Congress had granted regulatory, but not censorship, power over the public airwaves, investigated the complaint and, in an Order dated February 21, 1975, called the language used in Carlin's *Filthy Words* "offensive, indecent, vulgar, and shocking." The Order threatened sanctions against Pacifica, including fines or license revocation, if future complaints were received.

Pacifica appealed the FCC's Order to the U.S. Court of Appeals, which on March 16, 1977 struck it down. The FCC appealed for a reversal to the United States Supreme Court.

On July 3, 1978 the 5-4 decision of the Court was announced by Associate Justice John Paul Stevens.

The *Seven Words* Court

Chief Justice Warren Burger
Appointed Chief Justice by President Nixon
Served 1969 - 1986

Associate Justice William Brennan
Appointed by President Eisenhower
Served 1956 - 1990

Associate Justice Potter Stewart
Appointed by President Eisenhower
Served 1958 - 1981

Associate Justice Byron White
Appointed by President Kennedy
Served 1962 - 1993

Associate Justice Thurgood Marshall
Appointed by President Lyndon Johnson
Served 1967 - 1991

Associate Justice Harry Blackmun
Appointed by President Nixon
Served 1970 - 1994

Associate Justice Lewis Powell
Appointed by President Nixon
Served 1971 - 1987

Associate Justice William Rehnquist
Appointed by President Nixon
Served 1971 -

Associate Justice John Paul Stevens
Appointed by President Ford
Served 1975 -

The unedited text of *FCC v. Pacifica Foundation* can be found in volume 438 of *United States Reports*. Our edited plain-English text follows. George Carlin's *Filthy Words* is reproduced verbatim on page 132 of this book.

FCC v. PACIFICA FOUNDATION
July 3, 1978

JUSTICE JOHN PAUL STEVENS: This case requires that we decide whether the Federal Communications Commission has any power to regulate a radio broadcast that is indecent but not obscene.

A satiric humorist named George Carlin recorded a twelve-minute monologue entitled "Filthy Words" before a live audience in a California theater. He began by referring to his thoughts about "the words you couldn't say on the public, ah, airwaves, um, the ones you definitely wouldn't say, ever." He proceeded to list those words and repeat them over and over again in a variety of colloquialisms. The transcript of the recording, which is appended to this opinion, indicates frequent laughter from the audience.

At about 2 o'clock in the afternoon on Tuesday, October 30, 1973, a New York radio station, owned by respondent Pacifica Foundation, broadcast the "Filthy Words" monologue. A few weeks later a man, who stated that he had heard the broadcast while driving with his young son, wrote a letter complaining to the Commission. He stated that, although he could perhaps understand the "record's being sold for private use, I certainly cannot understand the broadcast of same over the air that, supposedly, you control."

The complaint was forwarded to the station for comment. In its response, Pacifica explained that the monologue had been played during a program about contemporary society's attitude toward language and that, immediately before its broadcast, listeners had been advised that it included "sensitive language which might be regarded as offensive to some." Pacifica characterized George Carlin as "a significant social satirist" who "like Twain and Sahl before him, examines the language of ordinary people. . . . Carlin is not mouthing obscenities, he is merely using words to satirize as harmless and essentially silly our attitudes towards those words." Pacifica stated that it was not aware of any other complaints about the broadcast.

On February 21, 1975, the Commission . . . [held] that Pacifica "could have been the subject of administrative sanctions." The Commission did not impose formal sanctions, but it did state that . . . "in the event that subsequent complaints are received, the Commission will then decide whether it should utilize any of the available sanctions it has been granted by Congress."

In its . . . opinion the Commission stated that it intended to "clarify the standards which will be utilized in considering" the growing number of complaints about indecent speech on the airwaves. Advancing several reasons for treating broadcast speech differently from other forms of expression, the Commission found a power to regulate indecent broadcasting in two statutes - Title 18, Section 1464 of the U.S. Code [the obscenity section], which forbids the use of "any obscene, indecent, or profane language by means of radio communications," and Title 47, Section 303(g) of the U.S. Code, which requires the Commission to "encourage the larger and more effective use of radio in the public interest."

The Commission characterized the language used in the Carlin monologue as "patently offensive," though not necessarily obscene, and expressed the opinion that it should be regulated by principles analogous to those found in the law of nuisance where the "law generally speaks to channeling behavior more than actually prohibiting it. . . . [T]he concept of 'indecent' is intimately connected with the exposure of children to language that describes, in terms patently offensive as measured by contemporary community standards for the broadcast medium, sexual or excretory activities and organs, at times of the day when there is a reasonable risk that children may be in the audience."

Applying these considerations to the language used in the monologue as broadcast by [Pacifica], the Commission concluded that certain words depicted sexual and excretory activities in a patently offensive manner, noted that they "were broadcast at a time when children were undoubtedly in the audience (i.e., in the early afternoon)," and that the prerecorded language, with those offensive words "repeated over and over," was "deliberately broadcast." In summary, the Commission stated, "We therefore hold that the language as broadcast was indecent and prohibited by [the obscenity section]."

. . . [T]he Commission was asked to clarify its opinion by ruling that the broadcast of indecent words as part of a live newscast would not be prohibited. The Commission issued another opinion in which it pointed out that it "never intended to place an absolute prohibition on the broadcast of this type of language, but rather sought to channel it to times of day when children most likely would not be exposed to it." The Commission . . . declined to comment on various hypothetical situations presented by the petition. It relied on its "long-standing policy of refusing to issue interpretive rulings or advisory opinions when the critical facts are not explicitly stated or there is a possibility that subsequent events will alter them."

The United States Court of Appeals for the District of Columbia Circuit reversed, with each of the three judges on the panel writing separately. Judge Tamm concluded that the order represented censorship and was expressly prohibited by Section 326 [the censorship section] of the Communications Act. Alternatively, Judge Tamm read the

Commission opinion as the functional equivalent of a rule and concluded that it was "overbroad." Chief Judge Bazelon's concurrence rested on the Constitution. . . . [H]e concluded that [the obscenity section] must be narrowly construed [interpreted] to cover only language that is obscene or otherwise unprotected by the First Amendment. Judge Leventhal, in dissent, stated that the only issue was whether the Commission could regulate the language "as broadcast." Emphasizing the interest in protecting children, not only from exposure to indecent language, but also from exposure to the idea that such language has official approval, he concluded that the Commission had correctly condemned the daytime broadcast as indecent.

Having granted the Commission's petition for certiorari [agreed to hear the case], we must decide - (1) whether the scope of judicial review encompasses more than the Commission's determination that the monologue was indecent "as broadcast"; (2) whether the Commission's order was a form of censorship forbidden by [the censorship section]; (3) whether the broadcast was indecent within the meaning of [the obscenity section]; and (4) whether the order violates the First Amendment of the United States Constitution.

The general statements in the Commission's . . . opinion do not change the character of its order. . . . The order "was issued in a specific factual context." . . . The specific holding was carefully confined to the monologue "as broadcast." . . . [T]he focus of our review must be on the Commission's determination that the Carlin monologue was indecent as broadcast.

The relevant statutory questions are whether the Commission's action is forbidden "censorship" within the meaning of [the censorship section] and whether speech that concededly is not obscene may be restricted as "indecent" under the authority of [the obscenity section]. The questions are not unrelated, for the two statutory provisions have a common origin. Nevertheless, we analyze them separately.

Section 29 of the Radio Act of 1927 provided,

> "Nothing in this Act shall be understood or construed to give the licensing authority the power of censorship over the radio communications or signals transmitted by any radio station, and no regulation or condition shall be promulgated or fixed by the licensing authority which shall interfere with the right of free speech by means of radio communications. No person within the jurisdiction of the United States shall utter any obscene, indecent, or profane language by means of radio communication."

The prohibition against censorship unequivocally denies the Commission any power to edit proposed broadcasts in advance and to excise material considered inappropriate for the airwaves. The prohibition, however, has never been construed to deny the Commission the power to review the content of completed broadcasts in the performance of its regulatory duties.

During the period between the original enactment of the provision in 1927 and its re-enactment in the Communications Act of 1934, the courts and the Federal Radio Commission held that the section deprived the Commission of the power to subject "broadcasting matter to scrutiny prior to its release," but they concluded that the Commission's "undoubted right" to take note of past program content when considering a licensee's renewal application "is not censorship."

Not only did the Federal Radio Commission so construe the statute prior to 1934; its successor, the Federal Communications Commission, has consistently interpreted the provision in the same way ever since. And, until this case, the Court of Appeals for the District of Columbia Circuit has consistently agreed with this construction. Thus, for example, in his opinion in *Anti-Defamation League of B'nai B'rith v. FCC*, Judge Wright forcefully pointed out that the Commission is not prevented from cancelling the license of a broadcaster who persists in a course of improper programming. He explained, "This would not be prohibited 'censorship,' . . . any more than would the Commission's considering on a license renewal application whether a broadcaster allowed 'coarse, vulgar, suggestive, double-meaning' programming; programs containing such material are grounds for denial of a license renewal."

Entirely apart from the fact that the subsequent review of program content is not the sort of censorship at which the statute was directed, its history makes it perfectly clear that it was not intended to limit the Commission's power to regulate the broadcast of obscene, indecent, or profane language. A single section of the 1927 Act is the source of both the anticensorship provision and the Commission's authority to impose sanctions for the broadcast of indecent or obscene language. Quite plainly, Congress intended to give meaning to both provisions. Respect for that intent requires that the censorship language be read as inapplicable to the prohibition on broadcasting obscene, indecent, or profane language.

There is nothing in the legislative history to contradict this conclusion. The provision was discussed only in generalities when it was first enacted. In 1934, the anticensorship provision and the prohibition against indecent broadcasts were re-enacted in the same section, just as in the 1927 Act. In 1948, when the Criminal Code was revised to include provisions that had previously been located in other Titles of the United States Code, the prohibition against obscene, indecent, and profane broadcasts was removed from the Communications Act and re-enacted as [the obscenity section]. That rearrangement of the Code cannot reasonably be interpreted as having been intended to change the meaning of the anticensorship provision.

We conclude, therefore, that [the censorship section] does not limit the Commission's authority to impose sanctions on licensees who engage in obscene, indecent, or profane broadcasting.

The only other statutory question presented by this case is whether the afternoon broadcast of the "Filthy Words" monologue was indecent within the meaning of [the obscenity section]. . . .

The Commission identified several words that referred to excretory or sexual activities or organs, stated that the repetitive, deliberate use of those words in an afternoon broadcast when children are in the audience was patently offensive, and held that the broadcast was indecent. Pacifica takes issue with the Commission's definition of indecency, but . . . does not quarrel with the conclusion that this afternoon broadcast was patently offensive. Pacifica's claim that the broadcast was not indecent within the meaning of the statute rests entirely on the absence of prurient appeal.

The plain language of the statute does not support Pacifica's argument. The words "obscene, indecent, or profane" are written in the disjunctive, implying that each has a separate meaning. Prurient appeal is an element of the obscene, but the normal definition of "indecent" merely refers to nonconformance with accepted standards of morality.

. . . . Because neither our prior decisions nor the language or history of [the obscenity section] supports the conclusion that prurient appeal is an essential component of indecent language, we reject Pacifica's construction of the statute.

When that construction is put to one side, there is no basis for disagreeing with the Commission's conclusion that indecent language was used in this broadcast.

Pacifica makes two constitutional attacks on the Commission's order. First, it argues that the Commission's construction of the statutory language broadly encompasses so much constitutionally protected speech that reversal is required even if Pacifica's broadcast of the "Filthy Words" monologue is not itself protected by the First Amendment. Second, Pacifica argues that inasmuch as the recording is not obscene, the Constitution forbids any abridgment of the right to broadcast it on the radio.

The first argument fails because our review is limited to the question whether the Commission has the authority to proscribe [prohibit] this particular broadcast. As the Commission itself emphasized, its order was "issued in a specific factual context." That approach is appropriate for courts as well as the Commission when regulation of indecency is at stake, for indecency is largely a function of context - it cannot be adequately judged in the abstract.

The approach is also consistent with *Red Lion Broadcasting Co. v. FCC.* In that case, the Court rejected an argument that the Commission's regulations defining the fairness doctrine were so vague that they would inevitably abridge the broadcasters' freedom of speech. The Court of Appeals had invalidated the regulations because their vagueness might lead to self-censorship of controversial program content. This Court reversed. After noting that the Commission had indicated, as it has in this case, that it would not impose sanctions without warning in cases in which the applicability of the law was unclear, the Court stated, "We need not approve every aspect of the fairness doctrine to decide these cases, and we will not now pass upon the constitutionality of these regulations by envisioning the most extreme applications conceivable, but will deal with those problems if and when they arise."

It is true that the Commission's order may lead some broadcasters to censor themselves. At most, however, the Commission's definition of indecency will deter only the broadcasting of patently offensive references to excretory and sexual organs and activities. While some of these references may be protected, they surely lie at the periphery of First Amendment concern. The danger dismissed so summarily in *Red Lion*, in contrast, was that broadcasters would respond to the vagueness of the regulations by refusing to present programs dealing with important social and political controversies. Invalidating any rule on the basis of its hypothetical application to situations not before the Court is "strong medicine" to be applied "sparingly and only as a last resort." We decline to administer that medicine to preserve the vigor of patently offensive sexual and excretory speech.

When the issue is narrowed to the facts of this case, the question is whether the First Amendment denies government any power to restrict the public broadcast of indecent language in any circumstances. For if the government has any such power, this was an appropriate occasion for its exercise.

The words of the Carlin monologue are unquestionably "speech" within the meaning of the First Amendment. It is equally clear that the Commission's objections to the broadcast were based in part on its content. The order must therefore fall if, as Pacifica argues, the First Amendment prohibits all governmental regulation that depends on the content of speech. Our past cases demonstrate, however, that no such absolute rule is mandated by the Constitution.

The classic exposition of the proposition that both the content and the context of speech are critical elements of

First Amendment analysis is Justice Holmes' statement for the Court in *Schenck v. United States,*

> "We admit that in many places and in ordinary times the defendants in saying all that was said in the circular would have been within their constitutional rights. But the character of every act depends upon the circumstances in which it is done. . . . The most stringent protection of free speech would not protect a man in falsely shouting fire in a theatre and causing a panic. It does not even protect a man from an injunction [court order stopping an action] against uttering words that may have all the effect of force. . . . The question in every case is whether the words used are used in such circumstances and are of such a nature as to create a clear and present danger that they will bring about the substantive evils that Congress has a right to prevent."

Other distinctions based on content have been approved in the years since *Schenck.* The government may forbid speech calculated to provoke a fight. It may pay heed to the "'commonsense differences' between commercial speech and other varieties." It may treat libels against private citizens more severely than libels against public officials. Obscenity may be wholly prohibited. And only two Terms ago we refused to hold that a "statutory classification is unconstitutional because it is based on the content of communication protected by the First Amendment."

The question in this case is whether a broadcast of patently offensive words dealing with sex and excretion may be regulated because of its content. Obscene materials have been denied the protection of the First Amendment because their content is so offensive to contemporary moral standards. But the fact that society may find speech offensive is not a sufficient reason for suppressing it. Indeed, if it is the speaker's opinion that gives offense, that consequence is a reason for according it constitutional protection. For it is a central tenet of the First Amendment that the government must remain neutral in the marketplace of ideas. If there were any reason to believe that the Commission's characterization of the Carlin monologue as offensive could be traced to its political content - or even to the fact that it satirized contemporary attitudes about four-letter words - First Amendment protection might be required. But that is simply not this case. These words offend for the same reasons that obscenity offends. Their place in the hierarchy of First Amendment values was aptly sketched by Justice Murphy when he said, "[S]uch utterances are no essential part of any exposition of ideas, and are of such slight social value as a step to truth that any benefit that may be derived from them is clearly outweighed by the social interest in order and morality."

Although these words ordinarily lack literary, political, or scientific value, they are not entirely outside the protection of the First Amendment. Some uses of even the most offensive words are unquestionably protected. Indeed, we may assume, [for the sake of argument,] that this monologue would be protected in other contexts. Nonetheless, the constitutional protection accorded to a communication containing such patently offensive sexual and excretory language need not be the same in every context. It is a characteristic of speech such as this that both its capacity to offend and its "social value," to use Justice Murphy's term, vary with the circumstances. Words that are commonplace in one setting are shocking in another. To paraphrase Justice Harlan, one occasion's lyric is another's vulgarity.

In this case it is undisputed that the content of Pacifica's broadcast was "vulgar," "offensive," and "shocking." Because content of that character is not entitled to absolute constitutional protection under all circumstances, we must consider its context in order to determine whether the Commission's action was constitutionally permissible.

We have long recognized that each medium of expression presents special First Amendment problems. And of all forms of communication, it is broadcasting that has received the most limited First Amendment protection. Thus, although other speakers cannot be licensed except under laws that carefully define and narrow official discretion, a broadcaster may be deprived of his license and his forum if the Commission decides that such an action would serve "the public interest, convenience, and necessity." Similarly, although the First Amendment protects newspaper publishers from being required to print the replies of those whom they criticize, it affords no such protection to broadcasters; on the contrary, they must give free time to the victims of their criticism.

The reasons for these distinctions are complex, but two have relevance to the present case. First, the broadcast media have established a uniquely pervasive presence in the lives of all Americans. Patently offensive, indecent material presented over the airwaves confronts the citizen, not only in public, but also in the privacy of the home, where the individual's right to be left alone plainly outweighs the First Amendment rights of an intruder. Because the broadcast audience is constantly tuning in and out, prior warnings cannot completely protect the listener or viewer from unexpected program content. To say that one may avoid further offense by turning off the radio when he hears indecent language is like saying that the remedy for an assault is to run away after the first blow. One may hang up on an indecent phone call, but that option does not give the caller a constitutional immunity or avoid a harm that has already taken place.

Second, broadcasting is uniquely accessible to children, even those too young to read. Although [a] written message might have been incomprehensible to a first grader, Pacifica's broadcast could have enlarged a child's vocabulary in an instant. Other forms of offensive expression may be withheld from the young without restricting the expression at its source. Bookstores and motion picture theaters, for example, may be prohibited from making indecent material available to children. We held in *Ginsberg v. New York* that the government's interest in the "well-being of its youth" and in supporting "parents' claim to authority in their own household" justified the regulation of otherwise protected expression. The ease with which children may obtain access to broadcast material, coupled with the concerns recognized in *Ginsberg*, amply justify special treatment of indecent broadcasting.

It is appropriate, in conclusion, to emphasize the narrowness of our holding. This case does not involve a two-way radio conversation between a cab driver and a dispatcher, or a telecast of an Elizabethan comedy. We have not decided that an occasional expletive in either setting would justify any sanction or, indeed, that this broadcast would justify a criminal prosecution. The Commission's decision rested entirely on a nuisance rationale under which context is all-important. The concept requires consideration of a host of variables. The time of day was emphasized by the Commission. The content of the program in which the language is used will also affect the composition of the audience, and differences between radio, television, and perhaps closed-circuit transmissions, may also be relevant. As Justice Sutherland wrote, a "nuisance may be merely a right thing in the wrong place - like a pig in the parlor instead of the barnyard." We simply hold that when the Commission finds that a pig has entered the parlor, the exercise of its regulatory power does not depend on proof that the pig is obscene.

The judgment of the Court of Appeals is reversed.

APPENDIX TO OPINION OF THE COURT

The following is a verbatim transcript of "Filthy Words" prepared by the Federal Communications Commission:

Aruba-du, ruba-tu, ruba-tu. I was thinking about the curse words and the swear words, the cuss words and the words that you can't say, that you're not supposed to say all the time, [']cause words or people into words want to hear your words. Some guys like to record your words and sell them back to you if they can, (laughter) listen in on the telephone, write down what words you say. A guy who used to be in Washington knew that his phone was tapped, used to answer, Fuck Hoover, yes, go ahead. (laughter) Okay, I was thinking one night about the words you couldn't say on the public, ah, airwaves, um, the ones you definitely wouldn't say, ever, [']cause I heard a lady say bitch one night on television, and it was cool like she was talking about, you know, ah, well, the bitch is the first one to notice that in the litter Johnie right (murmur) Right. And, uh, bastard you can say, and hell and damn so I have to figure out which ones you couldn't and ever and it came down to seven but the list is open to amendment, and in fact, has been changed, uh, by now, ha, a lot of people pointed things out to me, and I noticed some myself. The original seven words were, shit, piss, fuck, cunt, cocksucker, motherfucker, and tits. Those are the ones that will curve your spine, grow hair on your hands and (laughter) maybe, even bring us, God help us, peace without honor (laughter) um, and a bourbon. (laughter) And now the first thing that we noticed was that word fuck was really repeated in there because the word motherfucker is a compound word and it's another form of the word fuck. (laughter) You want to be a purist it doesn't really - it can't be on the list of basic words. Also, cocksucker is a compound word and neither half of that is really dirty. The word - the half sucker that's merely suggestive (laughter) and the word cock is a half-way dirty word, 50% dirty - dirty half the time, depending on what half the time, depending on what you mean by it. (laughter) Uh, remember when you first heard it, like in sixth grade, you used to giggle. And the cock crowed three times, heh (laughter) the cock - three times. It's in the Bible, cock in the Bible. (laughter) And the first time you heard about a cock-fight, remember - What? Huh? naw. It ain't that, are you stupid? man. (laughter, clapping) It's chickens, you know, (laughter) Then you have the four-letter words from the old Anglo-Saxon fame. Uh, shit and fuck. The word shit, uh, is an interesting kind of word in that the middle class has never really accepted it and approved it. They use it like, crazy but it's not really okay. It's still a rude, dirty, old kind of gushy word. (laughter) They don't like that, but they say it, like, they say it like, a lady now in a middle-class home, you'll hear most of the time she says it as an expletive, you know, it's out of her mouth before she knows. She says, Oh shit oh shit, (laughter) oh shit. If she drops something, Oh, the shit hurt the broccoli. Shit. Thank you. (footsteps fading away) (papers ruffling)

Read it! (from audience)

Shit! (laughter) I won the Grammy, man, for the comedy album. Isn't that groovy? (clapping, whistling) (murmur) That's true. Thank you. Thank you man. Yeah. (murmur) (continuous clapping) Thank you man. Thank you. Thank you very much, man. Thank, no, (end of continuous clapping) for that and for the Grammy, man, [']cause (laughter) that's based on people liking it man, yeh, that's ah, that's okay man. (laughter) Let's let that go, man. I got my Grammy. I can let my hair hang down now, shit. (laughter) Ha! So! Now the word shit is okay for the man. At work you can say it like crazy. Mostly figuratively, Get that shit out of here, will ya? I don't want to see that shit anymore. I can't cut that shit, buddy. I've had that shit up to here. I think you're full of shit myself. (laughter) He don't know shit from Shinola. (laughter) you know that? (laughter) Always wondered how the Shinola people felt about that (laughter) Hi, I'm the new man from Shinola. (laughter) Hi, how are ya? Nice to see ya. (laughter) How are ya? (laughter) Boy, I don't know whether to shit or wind my watch. (laughter) Guess, I'll shit on my watch. (laughter) Oh, the shit is going to hid de fan. (laughter) Built like a brick shit-house. (laughter) Up, he's up shit's creek. (laughter) He's had it. (laughter) He hit me, I'm sorry. (laughter) Hot shit, holy shit, tough shit, eat shit, (laughter) shit-eating grin. Uh, whoever thought of that was ill. (murmur laughter) He had a shit-eating grin! He had a what? (laughter) Shit on a stick. (laughter) Shit in a handbag. I always like that. He ain't worth shit in a handbag. (laughter) Shitty. He acted real shitty. (laughter) You know what I mean? (laughter) I got the money back, but a real shitty attitude. Heh, he had a shit-fit. (laughter) Wow! Shit-fit. Whew! Glad I wasn't there. (murmur, laughter) All the animals - Bull shit, horse shit, cow shit, rat shit, bat shit. (laughter) First time I heard bat shit, I really came apart. A guy in Oklahoma, Boggs, said it, man. Aw! Bat shit. (laughter) Vera reminded me of that last night, ah (murmur). Snake shit, slicker than owl shit. (laughter) Get your shit together. Shit or get off the pot. (laughter) I got a shit-load of them. (laughter) I got a shit-pot full, all right. Shit-head, shit-heel, shit in your heart, shit for brains, (laughter) shit-face, heh (laughter) I always try to think how that could have originated; the first guy that said that. Somebody got drunk and fell in some shit, you know. (laughter) Hey, I'm shit-face. (laughter) Shit-face, today. (laughter) Anyway, enough of that shit. (laughter) The big one, the word fuck that's the one that hangs them up the most. [']Cause in a lot of cases that's the very act that hangs them up the most. So, it's natural that the word would, uh, have the same effect. It's a great word, fuck, nice word, easy word, cute word, kind of. Easy word to say. One syllable, short u. (laughter) Fuck. (Murmur) You know, it's easy. Starts with a nice soft sound fuh ends with a kuh. Right? (laughter) A little something for everyone. Fuck (laughter)

Good word. Kind of a proud word, too. Who are you? I am FUCK. (laughter) FUCK OF THE MOUNTAIN. (laughter) Tune in again next week to FUCK OF THE MOUNTAIN. (laughter) It's an interesting word too, [']cause it's got a double kind of a life - personality - dual, you know, whatever the right phrase is. It leads a double life, the word fuck. First of all, it means, sometimes, most of the time, fuck. What does it mean? It means to make love. Right? We're going to make love, yeh, we're going to fuck, yeh, we're going to fuck, yeh, we're going to make love. (laughter) we're really going to fuck, yeh, we're going to make love. Right? And it also means the beginning of life, it's the act that begins life, so there's the word hanging around with words like love, and life, and yet on the other hand, it's also a word that we really use to hurt each other with, man. It's a heavy. It's one that you have toward the end of the argument. (laughter) Right? (laughter) You finally can't make out. Oh, fuck you man. I said, fuck you. (laughter, murmur) Stupid fuck. (laughter) Fuck you and everybody that looks like you. (laughter) man. It would be nice to change the movies that we already have and substitute the word fuck for the word kill, wherever we could, and some of those movie cliches would change a little bit. Madfuckers still on the loose. Stop me before I fuck again. Fuck the ump, fuck the ump, fuck the ump, fuck the ump, fuck the ump. Easy on the clutch Bill, you'll fuck that engine again. (laughter) The other shit one was, I don't give a shit. Like it's worth something, you know? (laughter) I don't give a shit. Hey, well, I don't take no shit, (laughter) you know what I mean? You know why I don't take no shit? (laughter) [']Cause I don't give a shit. (laughter) If I give a shit, I would have to pack shit. (laughter) But I don't pack no shit cause I don't give a shit. (laughter) You wouldn't shit me, would you? (laughter) That's a joke when you're a kid with a worm looking out the bird's ass. You wouldn't shit me, would you? (laughter) It's an eight-year-old joke but a good one. (laughter) The additions to the list. I found three more words that had to be put on the list of words you could never say on television, and they were fart, turd and twat, those three. (laughter) Fart, we talked about, it's harmless. It's like tits, it's a cutie word, no problem. Turd, you can't say but who wants to, you know? (laughter) The subject never comes up on the panel so I'm not worried about that one. Now the word twat is an interesting word. Twat! Yeh, right in the twat. (laughter) Twat is an interesting word because it's the only one I know of, the only slang word applying to the, a part of the sexual anatomy that doesn't have another meaning to it. Like, ah, snatch, box, and pussy all have other meanings, man. Even in a Walt Disney movie, you can say, We're going to snatch that pussy and put him in a box and bring him on the airplane. (murmur, laughter) Everybody loves it. The twat stands alone, man, as it should. And two-way words. Ah, ass is okay providing you're riding into town on a religious feast day. (laughter) You can't say, up your ass. (laughter) You can say, stuff it! (murmur) There are certain things you can say it's weird but you can just come so close. Before I cut, I, uh, want to, ah, thank you for listening to my words, man, fellow, uh space travelers. Thank you man for tonight and thank you also. (clapping whistling)

Sexually Explicit Mail
Miller v. California

"Obscene" means that to the average person, applying contemporary standards, the predominant appeal of the matter, taken as a whole, is to prurient interest, i.e., a shameful or morbid interest in nudity, sex, or excretion, which goes substantially beyond customary limits of candor in description or representation of such matters, and which is utterly without redeeming social importance.

- California's Obscenity Law (1969)

On June 25, 1969 the California State Legislature, in a effort to fight the sale of sexually explicit materials, enacted an Obscenity Law. California's Obscenity Law criminalized the mailing of materials deemed under the law to be obscene. From that date on, anyone distributing prohibited sexually explicit materials to unwilling recipients, persons who had in no way indicated any desire to receive such materials, could be charged with a crime.

After the passage of California's Obscenity Law, Marvin Miller, a person involved in the pornography trade in Orange County, California, conducted a mass mailing of sexually explicit materials to sell "adult" books and films. Advertised were a book entitled *An Illustrated History of Pornography* and a film entitled *Marital Intercourse*. Two recipients of Miller's unsolicited sexually explicit mailing, a mother and son, complained to California authorities. Miller was charged with violating California's Obscenity Law.

Tried in Orange County Superior Court, Miller was found guilty of a misdemeanor for having violated California's Obscenity Law. Miller appealed for a reversal of his conviction to the Appellate Division of the Orange County Superior Court. That Court upheld his conviction. Miller appealed for a reversal to the United States Supreme Court.

On June 21, 1973 the 5-4 decision of the Court was announced by Chief Justice Warren Burger.

The *Miller* Court

Chief Justice Warren Burger
Appointed Chief Justice by President Nixon
Served 1969 - 1986

Associate Justice William O. Douglas
Appointed by President Franklin Roosevelt
Served 1939 - 1975

Associate Justice William Brennan
Appointed by President Eisenhower
Served 1956 - 1990

Associate Justice Potter Stewart
Appointed by President Eisenhower
Served 1958 - 1981

Associate Justice Byron White
Appointed by President Kennedy
Served 1962 - 1993

Associate Justice Thurgood Marshall
Appointed by President Lyndon Johnson
Served 1967 - 1991

Associate Justice Harry Blackmun
Appointed by President Nixon
Served 1970 - 1994

Associate Justice Lewis Powell
Appointed by President Nixon
Served 1971 - 1987

Associate Justice William Rehnquist
Appointed by President Nixon
Served 1971 -

The unedited text of *Miller v. California* can be found in volume 413 of *United States Reports*. Our edited plain-English text follows.

MILLER v. CALIFORNIA
June 21, 1973

CHIEF JUSTICE WARREN BURGER: This is one of a group of "obscenity-pornography" cases being reviewed by the Court in a re-examination of standards enunciated in earlier cases involving what Justice Harlan called "the intractable obscenity problem."

Appellant [Marvin Miller] conducted a mass mailing campaign to advertise the sale of illustrated books, euphemistically called "adult" material. After a jury trial, he was convicted of violating [California's Obscenity Law], a misdemeanor, by knowingly distributing obscene matter, and the Appellate Department, Superior Court of California, County of Orange, summarily affirmed [upheld] the judgment. . . . [Miller]'s conviction was specifically based on his conduct in causing five unsolicited advertising brochures to be sent through the mail in an envelope addressed to a restaurant in Newport Beach, California. The envelope was opened by the manager of the restaurant and his mother. They had not requested the brochures; they complained to the police.

The brochures advertise four books entitled "Intercourse," "Man-Woman," "Sex Orgies Illustrated," and "An Illustrated History of Pornography," and a film entitled "Marital Intercourse." While the brochures contain some descriptive printed material, primarily they consist of pictures and drawings very explicitly depicting men and women in groups of two or more engaging in a variety of sexual activities, with genitals often prominently displayed.

This case involves the application of a State's criminal obscenity statute to a situation in which sexually explicit materials have been thrust by aggressive sales action upon unwilling recipients who had in no way indicated any desire to receive such materials. This Court has recognized that the States have a legitimate interest in prohibiting dissemination or exhibition of obscene material when the mode of dissemination carries with it a significant danger of offending the sensibilities of unwilling recipients or of exposure to juveniles. It is in this context that we are called on to define the standards which must be used to identify obscene material that a State may regulate without infringing on the First Amendment as applicable to the States through the Fourteenth Amendment.

. . . [I]t is useful for us to focus on two of the landmark cases in the somewhat tortured history of the Court's obscenity decisions. In *Roth v. United States*, the Court sustained [upheld] a conviction under a federal statute punishing the mailing of "obscene, lewd, lascivious or filthy . . ." materials. The key to that holding was the Court's rejection of the claim that obscene materials were protected by the First Amendment. Five Justices joined in the opinion stating, "All ideas having even the slightest redeeming social importance - unorthodox ideas, controversial ideas, even ideas hateful to the prevailing climate of opinion - have the full protection of the [First Amendment] guaranties, unless excludable because they encroach upon the limited area of more important interests. But implicit in the history of the First Amendment is the rejection of obscenity as utterly without redeeming social importance. . . . This is the same judgment expressed by this Court in *Chaplinsky v. New Hampshire*,

". . . . There are certain well-defined and narrowly limited classes of speech, the prevention and punishment of which have never been thought to raise any Constitutional problem. These include the lewd and obscene. . . . It has been well observed that such utterances are no essential part of any exposition of ideas, and are of such slight social value as a step to truth that any benefit that may be derived from them is clearly outweighed by the social interest in order and morality. . . ."

We hold that obscenity is not within the area of constitutionally protected speech or press.

Nine years later, in *Memoirs v. Massachusetts*, the Court veered sharply away from the *Roth* concept and, with only three Justices in the plurality opinion, articulated a new test of obscenity. The plurality held that under the *Roth* definition, "as elaborated in subsequent cases, three elements must coalesce - it must be established that (a) the dominant theme of the material taken as a whole appeals to a prurient interest in sex; (b) the material is patently offensive because it affronts contemporary community standards relating to the description or representation of sexual matters; and (c) the material is utterly without redeeming social value." . . . [T]he *Memoirs* plurality went on to state, "The Supreme Judicial Court erred in holding that a book need not be 'unqualifiedly worthless before it can be deemed obscene.' A book cannot be proscribed [prohibited] unless it is found to be utterly without redeeming social value."

While *Roth* presumed "obscenity" to be "utterly without redeeming social importance," *Memoirs* required that to prove obscenity it must be affirmatively established that the material is "utterly without redeeming social value." Thus, even as they repeated the words of *Roth*, the *Memoirs* plurality produced a drastically altered test that called on the prosecution to prove a negative, i.e., that the material was "utterly without redeeming social value" - a burden virtually impossible to discharge under our criminal standards of proof. Such considerations caused Justice Harlan to wonder if the "utterly without redeeming social value" test had any meaning at all.

Apart from the initial formulation in the *Roth* case, no majority of the Court has at any given time been able to agree on a standard to determine what constitutes obscene, pornographic material subject to regulation under the States' police power. We have seen "a variety of views among the members of the Court unmatched in any other course of constitutional adjudication." This is not remarkable, for in the area of freedom of speech and press the courts must always remain sensitive to any infringement of genuinely serious literary, artistic, political, or scientific expression. This is an area in which there are few eternal verities.

The case we now review was tried on the theory that [California's Obscenity Law] . . . approximately incorporates the three-stage *Memoirs* test. But . . . no Member of the Court today supports the *Memoirs* formulation.

This much has been categorically settled by the Court, that obscene material is unprotected by the First Amendment. "The First and Fourteenth Amendments have never been treated as absolutes." We acknowledge, however, the inherent dangers of undertaking to regulate any form of expression. State statutes designed to regulate obscene materials must be carefully limited. As a result, we now confine the permissible scope of such regulation to works which depict or describe sexual conduct. That conduct must be specifically defined by the applicable state law, as written or authoritatively construed [interpreted]. A state offense must also be limited to works which, taken as a whole, appeal to the prurient interest in sex, which portray sexual conduct in a patently offensive way, and which, taken as a whole, do not have serious literary, artistic, political, or scientific value.

The basic guidelines for the trier of fact [judge or jury] must be: (a) whether "the average person, applying contemporary community standards" would find that the work, taken as a whole, appeals to the prurient interest; (b) whether the work depicts or describes, in a patently offensive way, sexual conduct specifically defined by the applicable state law; and (c) whether the work, taken as a whole, lacks serious literary, artistic, political, or scientific value. We do not adopt as a constitutional standard the "utterly without redeeming social value" test of *Memoirs v. Massachusetts*; that concept has never commanded the adherence of more than three Justices at one time. If a state law that regulates obscene material is thus limited, as written or [interpreted], the First Amendment values applicable to the States through the Fourteenth Amendment are adequately protected by the ultimate power of appellate courts to conduct an independent review of constitutional claims when necessary.

We emphasize that it is not our function to propose regulatory schemes for the States. That must await their concrete legislative efforts. It is possible, however, to give a few plain examples of what a state statute could define for regulation . . . : (a) [p]atently offensive representations or descriptions of ultimate sexual acts, normal or perverted, actual or simulated; (b) [p]atently offensive representations or descriptions of masturbation, excretory functions, and lewd exhibition of the genitals.

Sex and nudity may not be exploited without limit by films or pictures exhibited or sold in places of public accommodation any more than live sex and nudity can be exhibited or sold without limit in such public places. At a minimum, prurient, patently offensive depiction or description of sexual conduct must have serious literary, artistic, political, or scientific value to merit First Amendment protection. For example, medical books for the education of physicians and related personnel necessarily use graphic illustrations and descriptions of human anatomy. In resolving the inevitably sensitive questions of fact and law, we must continue to rely on the jury system, accompanied by the safeguards that judges, rules of evidence, presumption of innocence, and other protective features provide, as we do with rape, murder, and a host of other offenses against society and its individual members. . . .

Under the holdings announced today, no one will be subject to prosecution for the sale or exposure of obscene materials unless these materials depict or describe patently offensive "hard core" sexual conduct specifically defined by the regulating state law, . . . as written or [interpreted]. We are satisfied that these specific prerequisites will provide fair notice to a dealer in such materials that his public and commercial activities may bring prosecution. If the inability to define regulated materials with ultimate, god-like precision altogether removes the power of the States or the Congress to regulate, then "hard core" pornography may be exposed without limit to the juvenile, the passerby, and the consenting adult alike. . . .

It is certainly true that the absence, since *Roth*, of a single majority view of this Court as to proper standards for testing obscenity has placed a strain on both state and federal courts. But today, for the first time since *Roth* was decided in 1957, a majority of this Court has agreed on concrete guidelines to isolate "hard core" pornography from expression protected by the First Amendment. Now we may . . . attempt to provide positive guidance to federal and state courts alike.

This may not be an easy road, free from difficulty. But no amount of "fatigue" should lead us to adopt a convenient "institutional" rationale - an absolutist, "anything goes" view of the First Amendment - because it will lighten our burdens. "Such an abnegation of judicial supervision in this field would be inconsistent with our duty to uphold the constitutional guarantees." Nor should we remedy "tension between state and federal courts" by arbitrarily depriving the States of a power reserved to them under the Constitution, a power which they have enjoyed and exercised continuously from before the adoption of the First Amendment to this day. "Our duty admits of no 'substitute for facing up to the tough individual problems of constitutional judgment involved in every obscenity case.'"

Under a national Constitution, fundamental First Amendment limitations on the powers of the States do not vary from community to community, but this does not mean that there are, or should or can be, fixed, uniform national standards of precisely what appeals to the "prurient interest" or is "patently offensive." These are essentially questions of fact, and our nation is simply too big and too diverse for this Court to reasonably expect that such standards could be articulated for all fifty States in a single formulation, even assuming the prerequisite consensus exists. When triers of fact are asked to decide whether "the average person, applying contemporary community standards" would consider certain materials "prurient," it would be unrealistic to require that the answer be based on some abstract formulation. The adversary system, with lay jurors as the usual ultimate factfinders in criminal prosecutions, has historically permitted triers of fact to draw on the standards of their community, guided always by limiting instructions on the law. To require a State to structure obscenity proceedings around evidence of a national "community standard" would be an exercise in futility.

. . . . The jury [in this case] . . . was explicitly instructed that, in determining whether the "dominant theme of the material as a whole . . . appeals to the prurient interest," and, in determining whether the material "goes substantially beyond customary limits of candor and affronts contemporary community standards of decency," it was to apply "contemporary community standards of the State of California."

During the trial, both the prosecution and the defense assumed that the relevant "community standards" in making the factual determination of obscenity were those of the State of California, not some hypothetical standard of the entire United States of America. Defense counsel at trial never objected to the testimony of the State's expert on community standards or to the instructions of the trial judge on "statewide" standards. On appeal to the Appellate Department, . . . [Miller] for the first time contended that application of state, rather than national, standards violated the First and Fourteenth Amendments.

We conclude that neither the State's alleged failure to offer evidence of "national standards," nor the trial court's charge that the jury consider state community standards, were constitutional errors. Nothing in the First Amendment requires that a jury must consider hypothetical and unascertainable "national standards" when attempting to determine whether certain materials are obscene as a matter of fact. Chief Justice Warren pointedly commented in his dissent in *Jacobellis v. Ohio*,

> "It is my belief that, when the Court said in *Roth* that obscenity is to be defined by reference to 'community standards,' it meant community standards - not a national standard, as is sometimes argued. I believe that there is no provable 'national standard.' . . . At all events, this Court has not been able to enunciate one, and it would be unreasonable to expect local courts to divine one."

It is neither realistic nor constitutionally sound to read the First Amendment as requiring that the people of Maine or Mississippi accept public depiction of conduct found tolerable in Las Vegas, or New York City. People in different States vary in their tastes and attitudes, and this diversity is not to be strangled by the absolutism of imposed uniformity. As the Court made clear in *Mishkin v. New York*, the primary concern with requiring a jury to apply the standard of "the average person, applying contemporary community standards" is to be certain that, so far as material is not aimed at a deviant group, it will be judged by its impact on an average person, rather than a particularly susceptible or sensitive person - or indeed a totally insensitive one. We hold that the requirement that the jury evaluate the materials with reference to "contemporary standards of the State of California" serves this protective purpose and is constitutionally adequate.

. . . [I]n our view, to equate the free and robust exchange of ideas and political debate with commercial exploitation of obscene material demeans the grand conception of the First Amendment and its high purposes in the historic struggle for freedom. It is a "misuse of the great guarantees of free speech and free press. . . ." The First Amendment protects works which, taken as a whole, have serious literary, artistic, political, or scientific value, regardless of whether the government or a majority of the people approve of the ideas these works represent. "The protection given speech and press was fashioned to assure unfettered interchange of ideas for the bringing about of political and social changes desired by the people." But the public portrayal of hardcore sexual conduct for its own sake, and for the ensuing commercial gain, is a different matter.

There is no evidence, empirical or historical, that the stern nineteenth century American censorship of public distribution and display of material relating to sex in any way limited or affected expression of serious literary, artistic, political, or scientific ideas. On the contrary, it is beyond any question that the era following Thomas Jefferson to Theodore Roosevelt was an "extraordinarily vigorous period" not just in economics and politics, but in belles lettres and in "the outlying fields of social and political philosophies." We do not see the harsh hand of censorship of ideas - good or bad, sound or unsound - and "repression" of political liberty lurking in every state regulation of commercial exploitation of human interest in sex.

. . . . One can concede that the "sexual revolution" of recent years may have had useful byproducts in striking layers of prudery from a subject long irrationally kept from needed ventilation. But it does not follow that no regulation of patently offensive "hard core" materials is needed or permissible; civilized people do not allow unregulated access to heroin because it is a derivative of medicinal morphine.

In sum, we: (a) reaffirm the *Roth* holding that obscene material is not protected by the First Amendment; (b) hold that such material can be regulated by the States, subject to the specific safeguards enunciated above, without a showing that the material is "utterly without redeeming social value"; and (c) hold that obscenity is to be determined by applying "contemporary community standards," not "national standards." The judgment of the Appellate Department of the Superior Court, Orange County, California, is vacated [set aside] and the case remanded [returned] to that court for further proceedings not inconsistent with the First Amendment standards established by this opinion.

Pornography And Privacy
Stanley v. Georgia

Any person who shall knowingly have possession of any obscene matter shall be charged with a felony, and upon conviction, shall be punished by confinement in the State Penitentiary for not less than one year and no more than five years. - **Georgia's Obscenity Law (1968)**

In 1968 the Georgia State Legislature made the private possession of obscene materials a crime. The Atlanta Police, armed with a search warrant, entered the home of Robert Eli Stanley during an investigation into his alleged illegal gambling activities. No evidence of illegal gambling activities was found, but police did find three reels of eight-millimeter film in Stanley's bedroom. After viewing the films, the police arrested Stanley on a charge of violating Georgia's Obscenity Law.

Stanley was tried and convicted by a jury in Fulton County Superior Court for violating Georgia's Obscenity Law. On appeal to the Georgia Supreme Court, Stanley argued that even if the materials found by the police in his home were obscene under the law (a fact he did not deny), his First Amendment right to receive information (obscene or not, especially in the privacy of his own home) protected him from prosecution. On April 9, 1968 the Georgia Supreme Court rejected Stanley's argument, finding that "obscenity is not within the area of constitutionally protected speech or press." They denied his appeal for a reversal of his sentence.

Stanley argued that Georgia's Obscenity Law violated his Constitutional rights by punishing him for private possession of obscene matter in his own home. He appealed for a reversal to the United States Supreme Court.

On April 7, 1969 the 6-3 decision of the Court was announced by Associate Justice Thurgood Marshall.

The *Stanley* Court

Chief Justice Earl Warren
Appointed Chief Justice by President Eisenhower
Served 1953 - 1969

Associate Justice Hugo Black
Appointed by President Franklin Roosevelt
Served 1937 - 1971

Associate Justice William O. Douglas
Appointed by President Franklin Roosevelt
Served 1939 - 1975

Associate Justice John Marshall Harlan
Appointed by President Eisenhower
Served 1955 - 1971

Associate Justice William Brennan
Appointed by President Eisenhower
Served 1956 - 1990

Associate Justice Potter Stewart
Appointed by President Eisenhower
Served 1958 - 1981

Associate Justice Byron White
Appointed by President Kennedy
Served 1962 - 1993

Associate Justice Abe Fortas
Appointed by President Lyndon Johnson
Served 1965 - 1969

Associate Justice Thurgood Marshall
Appointed by President Lyndon Johnson
Served 1967 - 1991

The unedited text of *Stanley v. Georgia* can be found in volume 394 of *United States Reports*. Our edited plain-English text follows.

STANLEY v. GEORGIA
April 7, 1969

JUSTICE THURGOOD MARSHALL: An investigation of appellant [Robert Stanley]'s alleged bookmaking activities led to the issuance of a search warrant for [his] home. Under authority of this warrant, federal and state agents secured entrance. They found very little evidence of bookmaking activity, but, while looking through a desk drawer in an upstairs bedroom, one of the federal agents, accompanied by a state officer, found three reels of eight-millimeter film. Using a projector and screen found in an upstairs living room, they viewed the films. The state officer concluded that they were obscene and seized them. Since a further examination of the bedroom indicated that [Stanley] occupied it, he was charged with possession of obscene matter and placed under arrest. He was later indicted [charged] for "knowingly hav[ing] possession of . . . obscene matter" in violation of Georgia law. [He] was tried before a jury and convicted. The Supreme Court of Georgia affirmed [upheld]. We [agreed to hear the case].

[Stanley] raises several challenges to the validity of his conviction. We find it necessary to consider only one. [Stanley] argues . . . that the Georgia obscenity statute, insofar as it punishes mere private possession of obscene matter, violates the First Amendment, as made applicable to the States by the Fourteenth Amendment. For reasons set forth below, we agree that the mere private possession of obscene matter cannot constitutionally be made a crime.

The [lower] court . . . saw no valid constitutional objection to the Georgia statute, even though it extends further than the typical statute forbidding commercial sales of obscene material. It held that "[i]t is not essential to an indictment charging one with possession of obscene matter that it be alleged that such possession was 'with intent to sell, expose, or circulate the same.'" The State and [Stanley] both agree that the question here before us is whether "a statute imposing criminal sanctions upon the mere [knowing] possession of obscene matter" is constitutional. . . . Georgia [,however,] contends that, since "obscenity is not within the area of constitutionally protected speech or press," the States are free, subject to the limits of other provisions of the Constitution, to deal with it any way deemed necessary, just as they may deal with possession of other things thought to be detrimental to the welfare of their citizens. If the State can protect the body of a citizen, may it not, argues Georgia, protect his mind?

It is true that *Roth [v. United States]* does declare, seemingly without qualification, that obscenity is not protected by the First Amendment. That statement has been repeated in various forms in subsequent cases. However, neither *Roth* nor any subsequent decision of this Court dealt with the precise problem involved in the present case. Roth was convicted of mailing obscene circulars and advertising, and an obscene book, in violation of a federal obscenity statute. The defendant in a companion case, *Alberts v. California*, was convicted of "lewdly keeping for sale obscene and indecent books, and [of] writing, composing, and publishing an obscene advertisement of them. . . ." None of the statements cited by the Court in *Roth* for the proposition that "this Court has always assumed that obscenity is not protected by the freedoms of speech and press" were made in the context of a statute punishing mere private possession of obscene material; the cases cited deal for the most part with use of the mails to distribute objectionable material or with some form of public distribution or dissemination. Moreover, none of this Court's decisions subsequent to *Roth* involved prosecution for private possession of obscene materials. Those cases dealt with the power of the State and Federal Governments to prohibit or regulate certain public actions taken or intended to be taken with respect to obscene matter. Indeed, with one exception, we have been unable to discover any case in which the issue in the present case has been fully considered.

In this context, we do not believe that this case can be decided simply by citing *Roth*. *Roth* and its progeny certainly do mean that the First and Fourteenth Amendments recognize a valid governmental interest in dealing with the problem of obscenity. But the assertion of that interest cannot, in every context, be insulated from all constitutional protections. Neither *Roth* nor any other decision of this Court reaches that far. As the Court said in *Roth* itself,

> "[c]easeless vigilance is the watchword to prevent . . . erosion [of First Amendment rights] by Congress or by the States. The door barring federal and state intrusion into this area cannot be left ajar; it must be kept tightly closed and opened only the slightest crack necessary to prevent encroachment upon more important interests."

Roth and the cases following it discerned such an "important interest" in the regulation of commercial distribution of obscene material. That holding cannot foreclose an examination of the constitutional implications of a statute forbidding mere private possession of such material.

It is now well established that the Constitution protects the right to receive information and ideas. "This freedom [of speech and press] . . . necessarily protects the right to receive. . . ." This right to receive information and ideas, regardless of their social worth, is fundamental to our free society. Moreover, in the context of this case - a prosecution for mere possession of printed or filmed matter in the privacy of a person's own home - that right takes on an added dimension. For also fundamental is the right to be free, except in very limited circumstances, from unwanted governmental intrusions into one's privacy.

"The makers of our Constitution undertook to secure conditions favorable to the pursuit of happiness. They recognized the significance of man's spiritual nature, of his feelings and of his intellect. They knew that only a part of the pain, pleasure, and satisfactions of life are to be found in material things. They sought to protect Americans in their beliefs, their thoughts, their emotions, and their sensations. They conferred, as against the Government, the right to be let alone - the most comprehensive of rights and the right most valued by civilized man."

These are the rights that [Stanley] is asserting in the case before us. He is asserting the right to read or observe what he pleases - the right to satisfy his intellectual and emotional needs in the privacy of his own home. He is asserting the right to be free from state inquiry into the contents of his library. Georgia contends that [Stanley] does not have these rights, that there are certain types of materials that the individual may not read or even possess. Georgia justifies this assertion by arguing that the films in the present case are obscene. But we think that mere categorization of these films as "obscene" is insufficient justification for such a drastic invasion of personal liberties guaranteed by the First and Fourteenth Amendments. Whatever may be the justifications for other statutes regulating obscenity, we do not think they reach into the privacy of one's own home. If the First Amendment means anything, it means that a State has no business telling a man, sitting alone in his own house, what books he may read or what films he may watch. Our whole constitutional heritage rebels at the thought of giving government the power to control men's minds.

And yet, in the face of these traditional notions of individual liberty, Georgia asserts the right to protect the individual's mind from the effects of obscenity. We are not certain that this argument amounts to anything more than the assertion that the State has the right to control the moral content of a person's thoughts. To some, this may be a noble purpose, but it is wholly inconsistent with the philosophy of the First Amendment. As the Court said in *Kingsley International Pictures Corp. v. Regents,*

"[t]his argument misconceives what it is that the Constitution protects. Its guarantee is not confined to the expression of ideas that are conventional or shared by a majority. . . . And in the realm of ideas it protects expression which is eloquent no less than that which is unconvincing."

Nor is it relevant that obscene materials in general, or the particular films before the Court, are arguably devoid of any ideological content. The line between the transmission of ideas and mere entertainment is much too elusive for this Court to draw, if indeed such a line can be drawn at all. Whatever the power of the state to control public dissemination of ideas inimical to the public morality, it cannot constitutionally premise legislation on the desirability of controlling a person's private thoughts.

Perhaps recognizing this, Georgia asserts that exposure to obscene materials may lead to deviant sexual behavior or crimes of sexual violence. There appears to be little empirical basis for that assertion. But, more important, if the State is only concerned about printed or filmed materials inducing antisocial conduct, we believe that in the context of private consumption of ideas and information we should adhere to the view that "[a]mong free men, the deterrents ordinarily to be applied to prevent crime are education and punishment for violations of the law. . . ." Given the present state of knowledge, the State may no more prohibit mere possession of obscene matter on the ground that it may lead to antisocial conduct than it may prohibit possession of chemistry books on the ground that they may lead to the manufacture of homemade spirits.

It is true that in *Roth* this Court rejected the necessity of proving that exposure to obscene material would create a clear and present danger of antisocial conduct or would probably induce its recipients to such conduct. But that case dealt with public distribution of obscene materials and such distribution is subject to different objections. For example, there is always the danger that obscene material might fall into the hands of children, or that it might intrude upon the sensibilities or privacy of the general public. No such dangers are present in this case.

Finally, we are faced with the argument that prohibition of possession of obscene materials is a necessary incident to statutory schemes prohibiting distribution. That argument is based on alleged difficulties of proving an intent to distribute or in producing evidence of actual distribution. We are not convinced that such difficulties exist, but even if they did, we do not think that they would justify infringement of the individual's right to read or observe what he pleases. Because that right is so fundamental to our scheme of individual liberty, its restriction may not be justified by the need to ease the administration of otherwise valid criminal laws.

We hold that the First and Fourteenth Amendments prohibit making mere private possession of obscene material a crime. *Roth* and the cases following that decision are not impaired by today's holding. As we have said, the States retain broad power to regulate obscenity; that power simply does not extend to mere possession by the individual in the privacy of his own home. Accordingly, the judgment of the [lower] court . . . is reversed and the case is remanded [returned] for proceedings not inconsistent with this opinion.

Smut Peddling
Ginsberg v. New York

"Harmful to minors" means any description or representation, in whatever form, of nudity . . . when it predominantly appeals to the prurient, shameful, or morbid interest of minors and is patently offensive to prevailing standards in the adult community, . . . and is utterly without redeeming social importance for minors.

- New York State's Smut Peddling Law (1965)

The New York State Legislature, in a effort to stop the sale of pornography to persons under the age of seventeen, enacted a Smut Peddling Law. New York's Smut Peddling Law criminalized, with the threat of imprisonment upon conviction, the sale to a minor of any obscene material that the state defined as being "harmful to minors."

In October 1965 Sam Ginsberg, the owner of a Long Island, New York luncheonette, sold two "girlie magazines" to a sixteen-year-old boy. Police arrested Ginsberg for two violations of the State's Smut Peddling Law. Tried in Nassau County Court, Ginsberg was found guilty of selling obscene material harmful to minors to a person under the age of seventeen. He appealed for a reversal to the New York State Supreme Court, arguing that that the New York State Legislature had no right to define what materials were obscene for children and not for adults. The New York State Supreme Court upheld his conviction.

Ginsberg challenged the constitutionality of the Smut Peddling Law on the grounds that its different definitions of obscenity - one standard for an adult and another standard for a minor - violated a minor's First Amendment right to read. He appealed for a reversal to the United States Supreme Court.

On April 22, 1968 the 6-3 decision of the Court was announced by Associate Justice William Brennan.

The *Smut Peddling* Court

Chief Justice Earl Warren
Appointed Chief Justice by President Eisenhower
Served 1953 - 1969

Associate Justice Hugo Black
Appointed by President Franklin Roosevelt
Served 1937 - 1971

Associate Justice William O. Douglas
Appointed by President Franklin Roosevelt
Served 1939 - 1975

Associate Justice John Marshall Harlan
Appointed by President Eisenhower
Served 1955 - 1971

Associate Justice William Brennan
Appointed by President Eisenhower
Served 1956 - 1990

Associate Justice Potter Stewart
Appointed by President Eisenhower
Served 1958 - 1981

Associate Justice Byron White
Appointed by President Kennedy
Served 1962 - 1993

Associate Justice Abe Fortas
Appointed by President Lyndon Johnson
Served 1965 - 1969

Associate Justice Thurgood Marshall
Appointed by President Lyndon Johnson
Served 1967 - 1991

The unedited text of *Ginsberg v. New York* can be found in volume 390 of *United States Reports*. Our edited plain-English text follows.

GINSBERG v. NEW YORK
April 22, 1968

JUSTICE WILLIAM BRENNAN: This case presents the question of the constitutionality . . . of a New York criminal obscenity statute [the Smut-Peddling Law], which prohibits the sale to minors under seventeen years of age of material defined to be obscene on the basis of its appeal to them whether or not it would be obscene to adults.

Appellant [Sam Ginsberg] and his wife operate "Sam's Stationery and Luncheonette" in Bellmore, Long Island. They have a lunch counter, and, among other things, also sell magazines including some so-called "girlie" magazines. [Ginsberg] was [charged with two counts of selling to] a sixteen-year-old boy two "girlie" magazines on each of two dates in October 1965, in violation of Section 484-h [the sales to minors section] of the New York Penal Law. He was tried before a judge without a jury in Nassau County District Court and was found guilty on both counts. The judge found (1) that the magazines contained pictures which depicted female "nudity" in a manner defined in subsection 1 (b) [of the sales to minors section], that is "the showing of . . . female buttocks . . . with less than a full opaque covering, or the showing of the female breast with less than a fully opaque covering of any portion thereof below the top of the nipple . . . ," and (2) that the pictures were "harmful to minors" in that they had, within the meaning of subsection 1(f) [of the sales to minors section] "that quality of . . . representation . . . of nudity [which] . . . (i) predominantly appeals to the prurient, shameful or morbid interest of minors, and (ii) is patently offensive to prevailing standards in the adult community as a whole with respect to what is suitable material for minors, and (iii) is utterly without redeeming social importance for minors." He held that both sales to the sixteen-year-old boy therefore constituted the violation under [the sales to minors section] of "knowingly to sell . . . to a minor" under seventeen of "(a) any picture . . . which depicts nudity . . . and which is harmful to minors," and "(b) any . . . magazine . . . which contains . . . [such pictures] . . . and which, taken as a whole, is harmful to minors." The conviction was affirmed [upheld] without opinion by the Appellate Term, Second Department, of the Supreme Court. [Ginsberg] was denied leave to appeal to the New York Court of Appeals and then appealed to this Court. We affirm.

The "girlie" picture magazines involved in the sales here are not obscene for adults. But [the sales to minors section] does not bar [Ginsberg] from stocking the magazines and selling them to persons seventeen years of age or older, and therefore the conviction is not invalid under our decision in *Butler v. Michigan.*

Obscenity is not within the area of protected speech or press. . . . [Ginsberg]'s primary attack upon [the sales to minors section] is leveled at the power of the State to adapt [the test in] *Memoirs [v. Massachusetts]* . . . to define the material's obscenity on the basis of its appeal to minors, and thus exclude material so defined from the area of protected expression. He makes no argument that the magazines are not "harmful to minors" within the definition in subsection 1(f) [of the sales to minors section]. Thus "[n]o issue is presented . . . concerning the obscenity of the material involved."

The New York Court of Appeals "upheld the Legislature's power to employ variable concepts of obscenity"" in a case in which the same challenge to state power to enact such a law was also addressed to [the sales to minors section]. In sustaining [upholding] state power to enact the law, the Court of Appeals said [in *Bookcase, Inc. v. Broderick*],

"[M]aterial which is protected for distribution to adults is not necessarily constitutionally protected from restriction upon its dissemination to children. In other words, the concept of obscenity or of unprotected matter may vary according to the group to whom the questionable material is directed or from whom it is quarantined. Because of the State's exigent interest in presenting distribution to children of objectionable material, it can exercise its power to protect the health, safety, welfare and morals of its community by barring the distribution to children of books recognized to be suitable for adults."

[Ginsberg]'s attack is not that New York was without power to draw the line at age seventeen. Rather, his contention is the broad proposition that the scope of the constitutional freedom of expression secured to a citizen to read or see material concerned with sex cannot be made to depend upon whether the citizen is an adult or a minor. He accordingly insists that the denial to minors under seventeen of access to material condemned by [the sales to minors section], insofar as that material is not obscene for persons seventeen years of age or older, constitutes an unconstitutional deprivation of protected liberty.

We have no occasion in this case to consider the impact of the guarantees of freedom of expression upon the totality of the relationship of the minor and the State. It is enough for the purposes of this case that we inquire whether it was constitutionally impermissible for New York, insofar as [the sales to minors section] does so, to accord minors under seventeen a more restricted right than that assured to adults to judge and determine for themselves what sex material they may read or see. We conclude that we cannot say that the [Smut-Peddling Law] invades the area of freedom of expression constitutionally secured to minors.

[Ginsberg] argues that there is an invasion of protected rights under [the sales to minors section]. . . . We reject that argument. We do not regard New York's regulation in defining obscenity on the basis of its appeal to minors under seventeen as involving an invasion of such minors' constitutionally protected freedoms. Rather [the sales to minors section] simply adjusts the definition of obscenity "to social realities by permitting the appeal of this type of material to be assessed in terms of the sexual interests . . . " of such minors. That the State has power to make that adjustment seems clear, for we have recognized that even where there is an invasion of protected freedoms "the power of the state to control the conduct of children reaches beyond the scope of its authority over adults. . . . "

The well-being of its children is of course a subject within the State's constitutional power to regulate, and, in our view, two interests justify the limitations in [the sales to minors section] upon the availability of sex material to minors under seventeen, at least if it was rational for the legislature to find that the minors' exposure to such material might be harmful. First of all, constitutional interpretation has consistently recognized that the parents' claim to authority in their own household to direct the rearing of their children is basic in the structure of our society. "It is cardinal with us that the custody, care and nurture of the child reside first in the parents, whose primary function and freedom include preparation for obligations the state can neither supply nor hinder." The legislature could properly conclude that parents and others, teachers for example, who have this primary responsibility for children's well-being are entitled to the support of laws designed to aid discharge of that responsibility. Indeed, subsection 1(f) (ii) of [the sales to minors section] expressly recognizes the parental role in assessing sex-related material harmful to minors according "to prevailing standards in the adult community as a whole with respect to what is suitable material for minors." Moreover, the prohibition against sales to minors does not bar parents who so desire from purchasing the magazines for their children.

The State also has an independent interest in the well-being of its youth. The New York Court of Appeals squarely bottomed its decision on that interest in *Bookcase, Inc. v Broderick*. Judge Fuld, now Chief Judge Fuld, also emphasized its significance in the earlier case of *People v. Kahan*, which had struck down the first version of [the sales to minors section] on grounds of vagueness. In his concurring opinion, he said,

> "While the supervision of children's reading may best be left to their parents, the knowledge that parental control or guidance cannot always be provided and society's transcendent interest in protecting the welfare of children justify reasonable regulation of the sale of material to them. It is, therefore, altogether fitting and proper for a state to include in a statute designed to regulate the sale of pornography to children special standards, broader than those embodied in legislation aimed at controlling dissemination of such material to adults."

In *Prince v. Massachusetts*, this Court, too, recognized that the State has an interest "to protect the welfare of children" and to see that they are "safeguarded from abuses" which might prevent their "growth into free and independent well-developed men and citizens." The only question remaining, therefore, is whether the New York Legislature might rationally conclude, as it has, that exposure to the materials proscribed [prohibited] by [the sales to minors section] constitutes such an "abuse."

Section 484-e of the law states a legislative finding that the material condemned by [the sales to minors section] is "a basic factor in impairing the ethical and moral development of our youth and a clear and present danger to the people of the state." It is very doubtful that this finding expresses an accepted scientific fact. But obscenity is not protected expression and may be suppressed without a showing of the circumstances which lie behind the phrase "clear and present danger" in its application to protected speech. To sustain state power to exclude material defined as obscenity by [the sales to minors section] requires only that we be able to say that it was not irrational for the legislature to find that exposure to material condemned by the [Smut-Peddling Law] is harmful to minors. In *Meyer v. Nebraska*, we were able to say that children's knowledge of the German language "cannot reasonably be regarded as harmful." That cannot be said by us of minors' reading and seeing sex material. To be sure, there is no lack of "studies" which purport to demonstrate that obscenity is or is not "a basic factor in impairing the ethical and moral development of . . . youth and a clear and present danger to the people of the state." But the growing consensus of commentators is that "while these studies all agree that a causal link has not been demonstrated, they are equally agreed that a causal link has not been disproved either." We do not demand of legislatures "scientifically certain criteria of legislation." We therefore cannot say that [the sales to minors section], in defining the obscenity of material on the basis of its appeal to minors under seventeen, has no rational relation to the objective of safeguarding such minors from harm.

[Ginsberg] challenges subsections (f) and (g) of [the sales to minors section] as in any event void for vagueness. The attack on subsection (f) is that the definition of obscenity "harmful to minors" is so vague that an honest distributor of publications cannot know when he might be held to have violated [the sales to minors section]. But the New York Court of Appeals construed [interpreted] this definition to be "virtually identical to the Supreme Court's most recent statement of the elements of obscenity. The definition therefore gives "men in acting adequate notice of what is prohibited" and does not offend the requirements of due process.

As is required by *Smith v. California*, [the sales to minors section] prohibits only those sales made "knowingly." The challenge to the scienter [knowledge] requirement of subsection (g) centers on the definition of "knowingly" insofar as it includes "reason to know" or "a belief or ground for belief which warrants further inspection or inquiry of both - (i) the character and content of any material described herein which is reasonably susceptible of examination by the defendant, and (ii) the age of the minor, provided however, that an honest mistake shall constitute an excuse from liability hereunder if the defendant made a reasonable bona fide attempt to ascertain the true age of such minor."

As to (i), [the sales to minors section] was passed after the New York Court of Appeals decided *People v. Finkelstein*, which read the requirement of [knowledge] into New York's general obscenity statute, Section 1141 of the Penal Law. The constitutional requirement of [knowledge], in the sense of knowledge of the contents of material, rests on the necessity "to avoid the hazard of self-censorship of constitutionally protected material and to compensate for the ambiguities inherent in the definition of obscenity." The Court of Appeals in *Finkelstein* interpreted [the obscenity section] to require "the vital element of [knowledge]" and defined that requirement in these terms:

"A reading of the statute as a whole clearly indicates that only those who are in some manner aware of the character of the material they attempt to distribute should be punished. It is not innocent but calculated purveyance of filth which is exorcised. . . . "

[We reject Ginsberg's] challenge to provision (i); it is unnecessary for us to define further today "what sort of mental element is requisite to a constitutionally permissible prosecution."

[Ginsberg] also attacks provision (ii) as impermissibly vague. This attack however is leveled only at the proviso according the defendant a defense of "honest mistake" as to the age of the minor. [He] argues that "the [Smut-Peddling Law] does not tell the bookseller what effort he must make before he can be excused." The argument is wholly without merit. The proviso states expressly that the defendant must be acquitted [found innocent] on the ground of "honest mistake" if the defendant proves that he made "a reasonable bona fide attempt to ascertain the true age of such minor."

Affirmed.

The Book Banned In Boston
Fanny Hill v. Massachusetts

The erotic novel *Memoirs of a Woman of Pleasure,* commonly know as *Fanny Hill,* was written by John Cleland and first published in England around 1750. The story relates the life story, including the sexual experiences, of a young woman who is forced into a life of prostitution.

In 1963 G.P. Putnam & Sons published and offered for sale copies of *Fanny Hill.* The Commonwealth of Massachusetts, following the U.S. Supreme Court's definition of obscenity as being "utterly without redeeming social importance," asked the Commonwealth's Courts to declare *Fanny Hill* obscene under Massachusetts law so that *Our people might be spared the necessity of determining for themselves whether or not to read it.* Massachusetts put on trial not the publisher or the distributor but the book itself.

Suffolk County Superior Court entered *Fanny Hill* into evidence and portions were read into the record. The prosecution and defense both called upon expert testimony relating to the book's literary, historical, and social value. The trial judge found *Fanny Hill* to be obscene and ordered the total suppression of the book, declaring it to be *Without the protection of the First and Fourteenth Amendments to the Constitution of the United States.* An appeal from this decision was taken to the Massachusetts Supreme Judicial Court.

On April 22, 1965 the Massachusetts Supreme Judicial Court, in upholding the Superior Court's total suppression of *Fanny Hill,* said, *We do not interpret the "social importance" test as requiring that a book which appeals to prurient interest and is patently offensive must be unqualifiedly worthless before it can be deemed obscene.* An appeal was taken to the United States Supreme Court.

On March 21, 1966 the 6-3 decision of the Court was announced by Associate Justice William Brennan.

The *Fanny Hill* Court

Chief Justice Earl Warren
Appointed Chief Justice by President Eisenhower
Served 1953 - 1969

Associate Justice Hugo Black
Appointed by President Franklin Roosevelt
Served 1937 - 1971

Associate Justice William O. Douglas
Appointed by President Franklin Roosevelt
Served 1939 - 1975

Associate Justice Tom Clark
Appointed by President Truman
Served 1949 - 1967

Associate Justice John Marshall Harlan
Appointed by President Eisenhower
Served 1955 - 1971

Associate Justice William Brennan
Appointed by President Eisenhower
Served 1956 - 1990

Associate Justice Potter Stewart
Appointed by President Eisenhower
Served 1958 - 1981

Associate Justice Byron White
Appointed by President Kennedy
Served 1962 - 1993

Associate Justice Abe Fortas
Appointed by President Lyndon Johnson
Served 1965 - 1969

The unedited text of *Fanny Hill v. Massachusetts* can be found in volume 383 of *United States Reports*. Our edited plain-English text follows.

FANNY HILL v. MASSACHUSETTS
March 21, 1966

JUSTICE WILLIAM BRENNAN: This is an obscenity case in which *Memoirs of a Woman of Pleasure* (commonly known as *Fanny Hill*), written by John Cleland in about 1750, was [judged] obscene in a proceeding that put on trial the book itself, and not its publisher or distributor. The . . . suit [was] brought by the Attorney General of Massachusetts, pursuant to General Laws of Massachusetts, . . . to have the book declared obscene. [Massachusetts law] requires that the petition commencing the suit be "directed against [the] book by name" and that an order to show cause "why said book should not be judicially determined to be obscene" be published in a daily newspaper and sent by registered mail "to all persons interested in the publication." Publication of the order in this case occurred in a Boston daily newspaper, and a copy of the order was sent by registered mail to G. P. Putnam's Sons, alleged to be the publisher and copyright holder of the book.

. . . G. P. Putnam's Sons intervened in the proceedings in behalf of the book, but it did not claim the right provided . . . to have the issue of obscenity tried by a jury. At the hearing before a justice of the Superior Court, . . . the court received the book in evidence and also . . . heard the testimony of experts and accepted other evidence, such as book reviews, in order to assess the literary, cultural, or educational character of the book. This constituted the entire evidence, as neither side availed itself of the opportunity . . . to introduce evidence "as to the manner and form of its publication, advertisement, and distribution." The trial justice [found] *Memoirs* obscene and declared that the book "is not entitled to the protection of the First and Fourteenth Amendments to the Constitution of the United

States." . . . The Massachusetts Supreme Judicial Court [agreed]. We [agreed to hear the case]. . . .

The term "obscene" appearing in the Massachusetts statute has been interpreted by the Supreme Judicial Court to be as expansive as the Constitution permits - the "statute covers all material that is obscene in the constitutional sense." . . . [T]he sole question before the state courts was whether *Memoirs* satisfies the test of obscenity established in *Roth v. United States.*

We defined obscenity in *Roth* in the following terms - "[W]hether to the average person, applying contemporary community standards, the dominant theme of the material taken as a whole appeals to prurient interest." Under this definition, . . . three elements must coalesce - it must be established that (a) the dominant theme of the material taken as a whole appeals to a prurient interest in sex; (b) the material is patently offensive because it affronts contemporary community standards relating to the description or representation of sexual matters, and (c) the material is utterly without redeeming social value.

The Supreme Judicial Court purported to apply the *Roth* definition of obscenity and held all three criteria satisfied. . . . [R]eversal is required because the court misinterpreted the social value criterion. The court applied the criterion in this passage,

"It remains to consider whether the book can be said to be 'utterly without social importance.' We are mindful that there was expert testimony, much of which was strained, to the effect that *Memoirs* is a structural novel with literary merit; that the book displays a skill in characterization and a gift for comedy; that it plays a part in the history of the development of the English novel, and that it contains a moral, namely, that sex with love is superior to sex in a brothel. But the fact that the testimony may indicate this book has some minimal literary value does not mean it is of any social importance. We do not interpret the 'social importance' test as requiring that a book which appeals to prurient interest and is patently offensive must be unqualifiedly worthless before it can be deemed obscene."

The Supreme Judicial Court erred in holding that a book need not be "unqualifiedly worthless before it can be deemed obscene." A book cannot be proscribed [prohibited] unless it is found to be utterly without redeeming social value. This is so even though the book is found to possess the requisite prurient appeal and to be patently offensive. . . .

It does not necessarily follow . . . that a determination that *Memoirs* is obscene in the constitutional sense would be improper under all circumstances. On the premise . . . that *Memoirs* has the requisite prurient appeal and is patently offensive, but has only a minimum of social value, the circumstances of production, sale, and publicity are relevant in determining whether or not the publication or distribution of the book is constitutionally protected. Evidence that the book was commercially exploited for the sake of prurient appeal, to the exclusion of all other values, might justify the conclusion that the book was utterly without redeeming social importance. It is not that in such a setting the social value test is relaxed so as to dispense with the requirement that a book be utterly devoid of social value, but rather that . . . where the purveyor's sole emphasis is on the sexually provocative aspects of his publications, a court could accept his evaluation at its face value. In this proceeding, however, the courts were asked to judge the obscenity of *Memoirs* in the abstract, and the declaration of obscenity was neither aided nor limited by a specific set of circumstances of production, sale, and publicity. All possible uses of the book must therefore be considered, and the mere risk that the book might be exploited by panderers because it so pervasively treats sexual matters cannot alter the fact - given the view of the Massachusetts court attributing to *Memoirs* a modicum of literary and historical value - that the book will have redeeming social importance in the hands of those who publish or distribute it on the basis of that value.

Reversed.

Hardcore Films
Jacobellis v. Ohio

The Ohio State Legislature, in a effort to stop statewide traffic in pornographic materials, enacted an Obscenity Law. Ohio's Obscenity Law criminalized the exhibition of any obscene, lewd, or lascivious book, magazine, picture, photograph, or motion picture. The maximum penalty for violating the Obscenity Law was seven years imprisonment and/or a $2,000 fine. The definition of what constituted obscenity was left up to "contemporary community standards of decency."

Nico Jacobellis managed a movie theater in Cleveland Heights, Ohio. On November 13, 1959 the theater exhibited a French film entitled *The Lovers*. The film, ninety minutes in length, contained one explicit, three minute sex scene. *The Lovers* was shown in about 100 American cities, including two Ohio cities, without incident. In Cleveland Heights, authorities found it to be a violation of their *local* "contemporary community standards of decency." Jacobellis was arrested.

Charged with two violations of Ohio's Obscenity Law - one for possession and another for exhibition of an obscene motion picture - Jacobellis was tried in Cuyahoga County Court. Convicted on June 3, 1960, he was fined $2,500. Jacobellis appealed for a reversal. On May 25, 1961 the Ohio Court of Appeals refused his appeal. On January 17, 1962 the Ohio Supreme Court refused his appeal.

Arguing that *The Lovers* was not obscene under *American society's* "contemporary community standards of decency" and that his conviction for exhibiting the film was thus a violation of his First Amendment right to free expression, Jacobellis appealed to the United States Supreme Court.

On June 22, 1964 the 6-3 decision of the Court was announced by Associate Justice William Brennan.

The *Jacobellis* Court

Chief Justice Earl Warren
Appointed Chief Justice by President Eisenhower
Served 1953 - 1969

Associate Justice Hugo Black
Appointed by President Franklin Roosevelt
Served 1937 - 1971

Associate Justice William O. Douglas
Appointed by President Franklin Roosevelt
Served 1939 - 1975

Associate Justice Tom Clark
Appointed by President Truman
Served 1949 - 1967

Associate Justice John Marshall Harlan
Appointed by President Eisenhower
Served 1955 - 1971

Associate Justice William Brennan
Appointed by President Eisenhower
Served 1956 - 1990

Associate Justice Potter Stewart
Appointed by President Eisenhower
Served 1958 - 1981

Associate Justice Byron White
Appointed by President Kennedy
Served 1962 - 1993

Associate Justice Arthur Goldberg
Appointed by President Kennedy
Served 1962 - 1965

The unedited text of *Jacobellis v. Ohio* can be found in volume 378 of *United States Reports*. Our edited plain-English text follows.

JACOBELLIS v. OHIO
June 22, 1964

JUSTICE WILLIAM BRENNAN: Appellant, Nico Jacobellis, manager of a motion picture theater in Cleveland Heights, Ohio, was convicted on two counts of possessing and exhibiting an obscene film in violation of [the] Ohio Revised Code. . . . He was fined $500 on the first count and $2,000 on the second, and was sentenced to the workhouse if the fines were not paid. His conviction, by a court of three judges upon waiver of trial by jury, was affirmed [upheld] by an intermediate appellate court. We [agreed to hear the case]. The dispositive question is whether the state courts properly found that the motion picture involved, a French film called "Les Amants" ("The Lovers"), was obscene, and hence not entitled to the protection for free expression that is guaranteed by the First and Fourteenth Amendments. We conclude that the film is not obscene, and that the judgment must accordingly be reversed.

Motion pictures are within the ambit of the constitutional guarantees of freedom of speech and of the press. But in *Roth v. United States* and *Alberts v. California*, we held that obscenity is not subject to those guarantees. Application of an obscenity law to suppress a motion picture thus requires ascertainment of the "dim and uncertain line" that often separates obscenity from constitutionally protected expression. It has been suggested that this is a task in which our Court need not involve itself. We are told that the determination whether a particular motion picture, book, or other work of expression is obscene can be treated as a purely factual judgment on which a jury's verdict is all but conclusive, or that in any event the decision can be left essentially to state and lower federal courts, with this Court exercising only a limited review such as that needed to determine whether the ruling [of the lower courts] is supported by "sufficient evidence." The suggestion is appealing, since it would lift from our shoulders a difficult, recurring, and unpleasant task. But we cannot accept it. Such an abnegation of judicial supervision in this field would be inconsistent with our duty to uphold the constitutional guarantees. Since it is only "obscenity" that is excluded from the constitutional protection, the question whether a particular work is obscene necessarily implicates an issue of constitutional law. Such an issue, we think, must ultimately be decided by this Court. Our duty admits of no "substitute for facing up to the tough individual problems of constitutional judgment involved in every obscenity case."

In other areas involving constitutional rights under the Due Process Clause, the Court has consistently recognized its duty to apply the applicable rules of law upon the basis of an independent review of the facts of each case. And this has been particularly true where rights have been asserted under the First Amendment guarantees of free expression. . . .

We cannot understand why the Court's duty should be any different in the present case, where Jacobellis has been subjected to a criminal conviction for disseminating a work of expression and is challenging that conviction as a deprivation of rights guaranteed by the First and Fourteenth Amendments. Nor can we understand why the Court's performance of its constitutional and judicial function in this sort of case should be denigrated by such epithets as "censor" or "super-censor." In judging alleged obscenity, the Court is no more "censoring" expression than it has in other cases "censored" criticism of judges and public officials, advocacy of governmental overthrow, or speech alleged to constitute a breach of the peace. Use of an opprobrious label can neither obscure nor impugn the Court's performance of its obligation to test challenged judgments against the guarantees of the First and Fourteenth Amendments and, in doing so, to delineate the scope of constitutionally protected speech. Hence, we reaffirm the principle that, in "obscenity" cases, as in all others involving rights derived from the First Amendment guarantees of free expression, this Court cannot avoid making an independent constitutional judgment on the facts of the case as to whether the material involved is constitutionally protected.

The question of the proper standard for making this determination has been the subject of much discussion and controversy since our decision in *Roth* seven years ago. Recognizing that the test for obscenity enunciated there - "whether to the average person, applying contemporary community standards, the dominant theme of the material taken as a whole appeals to prurient interest" - is not perfect, we think any substitute would raise equally difficult problems, and we therefore adhere to that standard. We would reiterate, however, our recognition in *Roth* that obscenity is excluded from the constitutional protection only because it is "utterly without redeeming social importance," and that "the portrayal of sex, e.g., in art, literature, and scientific works, is not itself sufficient reason to deny material the constitutional protection of freedom of speech and press." It follows that material dealing with sex in a manner that advocates ideas, or that has literary or scientific or artistic value or any other form of social importance, may not be branded as obscenity and denied the constitutional protection. Nor may the constitutional status of the material be made to turn on a "weighing" of its social importance against its prurient appeal, for a work cannot be proscribed [prohibited] unless it is "utterly" without social importance. It should also be recognized that the *Roth* standard requires in the first instance a finding that the material "goes substantially beyond customary limits of candor in description or representation of such matters." This was a requirement of the Model Penal Code test that we approved in *Roth*, and it is explicitly reaffirmed in the more recent "Proposed Of-

ficial Draft" of the Code. In the absence of such a devia-
tion from society's standards of decency, we do not see how
any official inquiry into the allegedly prurient appeal of a
work of expression can be squared with the guarantees of
the First and Fourteenth Amendments.

It has been suggested that the "contemporary community
standards" aspect of the *Roth* test implies a determination
of the constitutional question of obscenity in each case by
the standards of the particular local community from which
the case arises. This is an incorrect reading of *Roth*. The
concept of "contemporary community standards" was first
expressed by Judge Learned Hand in *United States v. Kenner-
ley*, where he said,

> "Yet, if the time is not yet when men think innocent all
> that which is honestly germane to a pure subject, how-
> ever little it may mince its words, still I scarcely think that
> they would forbid all which might corrupt the most cor-
> ruptible, or that society is prepared to accept for its own
> limitations those which may perhaps be necessary to the
> weakest of its members. If there be no abstract defini-
> tion, such as I have suggested, should not the word
> 'obscene' be allowed to indicate the present critical point
> in the compromise between candor and shame at which
> the community may have arrived here and now? . . . To
> put thought in leash to the average conscience of the
> time is perhaps tolerable, but to fetter it by the necessi-
> ties of the lowest and least capable seems a fatal policy.

> "Nor is it an objection, I think, that such an interpreta-
> tion gives to the words of the statute a varying meaning
> from time to time. Such words as these do not embalm
> the precise morals of an age or place; while they presup-
> pose that some things will always be shocking to the
> public taste, the vague subject matter is left to the grad-

ual development of general notions about what is de-
cent. . . ."

It seems clear that in this passage Judge Hand was referring
not to state and local "communities," but rather to "the
community" in the sense of "society at large; . . . the public,
or people in general." Thus, he recognized that under his
standard the concept of obscenity would have "a varying
meaning from time to time" - not from county to county, or
town to town.

We do not see how any "local" definition of the
"community" could properly be employed in delineating the
area of expression that is protected by the Federal Constitution. Justice Harlan pointed out in *Manual Enterprises, Inc.,
v. Day* that a standard based on a particular local community
would have "the intolerable consequence of denying some
sections of the country access to material, there deemed
acceptable, which in others might be considered offensive
to prevailing community standards of decency."

It is true that *Manual Enterprises* dealt with the federal statute
banning obscenity from the mails. But the mails are not the
only means by which works of expression cross local community lines in this country. It can hardly be assumed that
all the patrons of a particular library, bookstand, or motion
picture theater are residents of the smallest local
"community" that can be drawn around that establishment.
Furthermore, to sustain [uphold] the suppression of a particular book or film in one locality would deter its dissemination in other localities where it might be held not obscene, since sellers and exhibitors would be reluctant to risk
criminal conviction in testing the variation between the two
places. It would be a hardy person who would sell a book or
exhibit a film anywhere in the land after this Court had
sustained the judgment of one "community" holding it to
be outside the constitutional protection. The result would

thus be "to restrict the public's access to forms of the printed word which the State could not constitutionally suppress directly."

It is true that local communities throughout the land are in fact diverse, and that in cases such as this one the Court is confronted with the task of reconciling the rights of such communities with the rights of individuals. Communities vary, however, in many respects other than their toleration of alleged obscenity, and such variances have never been considered to require or justify a varying standard for application of the Federal Constitution. The Court has regularly been compelled, in reviewing criminal convictions challenged under the Due Process Clause of the Fourteenth Amendment, to reconcile the conflicting rights of the local community which brought the prosecution and of the individual defendant [person accused of a crime]. Such a task is admittedly difficult and delicate, but it is inherent in the Court's duty of determining whether a particular conviction worked a deprivation of rights guaranteed by the Federal Constitution. The Court has not shrunk from discharging that duty in other areas, and we see no reason why it should do so here. The Court has explicitly refused to tolerate a result whereby "the constitutional limits of free expression in the Nation would vary with state lines"; we see even less justification for allowing such limits to vary with town or county lines. We thus reaffirm the position taken in *Roth* to the effect that the constitutional status of an allegedly obscene work must be determined on the basis of a national standard. It is, after all, a national Constitution we are expounding.

We recognize the legitimate and indeed exigent interest of States and localities throughout the Nation in preventing the dissemination of material deemed harmful to children. But that interest does not justify a total suppression of such material, the effect of which would be to "reduce the adult population . . . to reading only what is fit for children." State and local authorities might well consider whether their objectives in this area would be better served by laws aimed specifically at preventing distribution of objectionable material to children, rather than at totally prohibiting its dissemination. Since the present conviction is based upon exhibition of the film to the public at large and not upon its exhibition to children, the judgment must be reviewed under the strict standard applicable in determining the scope of the expression that is protected by the Constitution.

We have applied that standard to the motion picture in question. "The Lovers" involves a woman bored with her life and marriage who abandons her husband and family for a young archaeologist with whom she has suddenly fallen in love. There is an explicit love scene in the last reel of the film, and the State's objections are based almost entirely upon that scene. The film was favorably reviewed in a number of national publications, although disparaged in others, and was rated by at least two critics of national stature among the best films of the year in which it was produced. It was shown in approximately 100 of the larger cities in the United States, including Columbus and Toledo, Ohio.

We have viewed the film . . . and we conclude that it is not obscene within the standards enunciated in *Roth v. United States* and *Alberts v. California*, which we reaffirm here.

Reversed.

Utterly Without Redeeming Social Value
Roth v. United States
Alberts v. California

In 1872 Congress enacted a Federal Obscenity Law criminalizing the use of the mails for the sending of obscene materials - *Whoever knowingly deposits for mailing material declared obscene, lewd, or lascivious, shall be fined or imprisoned.*

Samuel Roth operated a pornographic publishing business in New York City. Roth was charged with violations of the Federal Obscenity Law. Tried and convicted in U.S. District Court, Roth appealed for a reversal to the U.S. Court of Appeals which, on January 14, 1957, upheld his conviction. Roth then appealed to the U.S. Supreme Court, arguing that the Federal Obscenity Law was an unconstitutional violation of his First Amendment free speech and free press rights.

In 1872 the California State Legislature enacted a State Obscenity Law criminalizing the selling of obscene and indecent materials - *Every person who willfully or lewdly advertises or sells any obscene and indecent writing is guilty of a misdemeanor.*

David Alberts operated a mail order pornography business in Beverly Hills, California. Alberts was charged with violations of California's Obscenity Law. Tried and convicted in Beverly Hills Municipal Court, Alberts appealed for a reversal to the Appellate Division of the Los Angles Superior Court which, on January 12, 1956, upheld his conviction. Alberts appealed to the United States Supreme Court, arguing that California's Obscenity Law was an unconstitutional violation of his First Amendment free speech and free press rights.

The Supreme Court combined the *Roth* and *Alberts* appeals.

On June 24, 1957 the 6-3 decision of the Court was announced by Associate Justice William Brennan.

The *Roth/Alberts* Court

Chief Justice Earl Warren
Appointed Chief Justice by President Eisenhower
Served 1953 - 1969

Associate Justice Hugo Black
Appointed by President Franklin Roosevelt
Served 1937 - 1971

Associate Justice Stanley Reed
Appointed by President Franklin Roosevelt
Served 1938 - 1957

Associate Justice Felix Frankfurter
Appointed by President Franklin Roosevelt
Served 1939 - 1962

Associate Justice William O. Douglas
Appointed by President Franklin Roosevelt
Served 1939 - 1975

Associate Justice Harold Burton
Appointed by President Truman
Served 1945 - 1958

Associate Justice Tom Clark
Appointed by President Truman
Served 1949 - 1967

Associate Justice John Marshall Harlan
Appointed by President Eisenhower
Served 1955 - 1971

Associate Justice William Brennan
Appointed by President Eisenhower
Served 1956 - 1990

The unedited text of *Roth v. United States* and *Alberts v. California* can be found in volume 354 of *United States Reports*. Our edited plain-English text follows.

ROTH v. UNITED STATES
ALBERTS v. CALIFORNIA
June 24, 1957

JUSTICE WILLIAM BRENNAN: The constitutionality of a criminal obscenity statute is the question in each of these cases. In *Roth*, the primary constitutional question is whether the federal obscenity statute violates the provision of the First Amendment that "Congress shall make no law . . . abridging the freedom of speech, or of the press. . . ." In *Alberts*, the primary constitutional question is whether the obscenity provisions of the California Penal Code invade the freedoms of speech and press as they may be incorporated in the liberty protected from state action by the Due Process Clause of the Fourteenth Amendment.

Other constitutional questions are: whether these statutes violate due process, because too vague to support conviction for crime; whether power to punish speech and press offensive to decency and morality is in the States alone, so that the federal obscenity statute violates the Ninth and Tenth Amendments (raised in *Roth*), and whether Congress, by enacting the federal obscenity statute, under the power delegated by Article I, Section 8, clause 7 [of the Constitution], to establish post offices and post roads, preempted the regulation of the subject matter (raised in *Alberts*).

[Samuel] Roth conducted a business in New York in the publication and sale of books, photographs, and magazines. He used circulars and advertising matter to solicit sales. He was convicted by a jury in the District Court for the Southern District of New York upon 4 counts of a 26-count indictment charging him with mailing obscene circulars and advertising, and an obscene book, in violation of the federal obscenity statute. His conviction was affirmed [upheld] by the Court of Appeals for the Second Circuit. We granted certiorari [agreed to hear the case].

[David] Alberts conducted a mail-order business from Los Angeles. He was convicted by the Judge of the Municipal Court of the Beverly Hills Judicial District (having waived a jury trial) under a misdemeanor complaint which charged him with lewdly keeping for sale obscene and indecent books, and with writing, composing, and publishing an obscene advertisement of them, in violation of the California Penal Code. The conviction was affirmed by the Appellate Department of the Superior Court of the State of California in and for the County of Los Angeles. . . .

The . . . question is whether obscenity is utterance within the area of protected speech and press. Although this is the first time the question has been squarely presented to this Court, either under the First Amendment or under the Fourteenth Amendment, expressions found in numerous opinions indicate that this Court has always assumed that obscenity is not protected by the freedoms of speech and press.

The guaranties of freedom of expression in effect in ten of the fourteen States which by 1792 had ratified the Constitution, gave no absolute protection for every utterance. Thirteen of the fourteen States provided for the prosecution of libel, and all of those States made either blasphemy or profanity, or both, statutory crimes. As early as 1712, Massachusetts made it criminal to publish "any filthy, obscene, or profane song, pamphlet, libel, or mock sermon" in imitation or mimicking of religious services. Thus, profanity and obscenity were related offenses.

In light of this history, it is apparent that the unconditional phrasing of the First Amendment was not intended to protect every utterance. This phrasing did not prevent this Court from concluding that libelous utterances are not within the area of constitutionally protected speech. At the time of the adoption of the First Amendment, obscenity law was not as fully developed as libel law, but there is sufficiently contemporaneous evidence to show that obscenity, too, was outside the protection intended for speech and press.

The protection given speech and press was fashioned to assure unfettered interchange of ideas for the bringing about of political and social changes desired by the people. This objective was made explicit as early as 1774 in a letter of the Continental Congress to the inhabitants of Quebec:

> "The last right we shall mention regards the freedom of the press. The importance of this consists, besides the advancement of truth, science, morality, and arts in general, in its diffusion of liberal sentiments on the administration of Government, its ready communication of thoughts between subjects, and its consequential promotion of union among them, whereby oppressive officers are shamed or intimidated into more honorable and just modes of conducting affairs."

All ideas having even the slightest redeeming social importance - unorthodox ideas, controversial ideas, even ideas hateful to the prevailing climate of opinion - have the full protection of the guaranties, unless excludable because they encroach upon the limited area of more important interests. But implicit in the history of the First Amendment is the rejection of obscenity as utterly without redeeming social importance. This rejection for that reason is mirrored in the universal judgment that obscenity should be restrained, reflected in the international agreement of over fifty nations, in the obscenity laws of all of the forty-eight States, and in the twenty obscenity laws enacted by the Congress from 1842 to 1956. This is the same judgment expressed by this Court in *Chaplinsky v. New Hampshire*:

> "There are certain well-defined and narrowly limited classes of speech, the prevention and punishment of which have never been thought to raise any Constitutional problem. These include the lewd and obscene. . . . It has been well observed that such utterances are no es-

sential part of any exposition of ideas, and are of such slight social value as a step to truth that any benefit that may be derived from them is clearly outweighed by the social interest in order and morality. . . ."

We hold that obscenity is not within the area of constitutionally protected speech or press.

It is strenuously urged that these obscenity statutes offend the constitutional guaranties because they punish incitation to impure sexual thoughts, not shown to be related to any overt antisocial conduct which is or may be incited in the persons stimulated to such thoughts. In *Roth*, the trial judge instructed the jury - "The words 'obscene, lewd, and lascivious' as used in the law, signify that form of immorality which has relation to sexual impurity and has a tendency to excite lustful thoughts." In *Alberts*, the trial judge applied the test laid down in *People v. Wepplo*, namely, whether the material has "a substantial tendency to deprave or corrupt its readers by inciting lascivious thoughts or arousing lustful desires." It is insisted that the constitutional guaranties are violated because convictions may be had without proof either that obscene material will perceptibly create a clear and present danger of anti-social conduct, or will probably induce its recipients to such conduct. But, in light of our holding that obscenity is not protected speech, the complete answer to this argument is in the holding of this Court in *Beauharnais v. Illinois*:

"Libelous utterances not being within the area of constitutionally protected speech, it is unnecessary, either for us or for the State courts, to consider the issues behind the phrase 'clear and present danger.' Certainly no one would contend that obscene speech, for example, may be punished only upon a showing of such circumstances. Libel, as we have seen, is in the same class."

However, sex and obscenity are not synonymous. Obscene material is material which deals with sex in a manner appealing to prurient interest. The portrayal of sex, e.g., in art, literature, and scientific works, is not itself sufficient reason to deny material the constitutional protection of freedom of speech and press. Sex, a great and mysterious motive force in human life, has indisputably been a subject of absorbing interest to mankind through the ages; it is one of the vital problems of human interest and public concern. As to all such problems, this Court said in *Thornhill v. Alabama*:

> "The freedom of speech and of the press guaranteed by the Constitution embraces at the least the liberty to discuss publicly and truthfully all matters of public concern without previous restraint or fear of subsequent punishment. The exigencies of the colonial period and the efforts to secure freedom from oppressive administration developed a broadened conception of these liberties as adequate to supply the public need for information and education with respect to the significant issues of the times. . . . Freedom of discussion, if it would fulfill its historic function in this nation, must embrace all issues about which information is needed or appropriate to enable the members of society to cope with the exigencies of their period."

The fundamental freedoms of speech and press have contributed greatly to the development and well-being of our free society and are indispensable to its continued growth. Ceaseless vigilance is the watchword to prevent their erosion by Congress or by the States. The door barring federal and state intrusion into this area cannot be left ajar; it must be kept tightly closed, and opened only the slightest crack necessary to prevent encroachment upon more important interests. It is therefore vital that the standards for judging obscenity safeguard the protection of freedom of speech and press for material which does not treat sex in a manner appealing to prurient interest.

The early leading standard of obscenity [in *Regina v. Hicklin*] allowed material to be judged merely by the effect of an isolated excerpt upon particularly susceptible persons. . . . Some American courts adopted this standard, but later decisions have rejected it and substituted this test - whether, to the average person, applying contemporary community standards, the dominant theme of the material, taken as a whole appeals to prurient interest. The *Hicklin* test, judging obscenity by the effect of isolated passages upon the most susceptible persons, might well encompass material legitimately treating with sex, and so it must be rejected as unconstitutionally restrictive of the freedoms of speech and press. On the other hand, the substituted standard provides safeguards adequate to withstand the charge of constitutional infirmity.

Both [lower] trial courts . . . sufficiently followed the proper standard. Both courts used the proper definition of obscenity. In addition, in the *Alberts* case, . . . the trial judge indicated that, as the trier of facts, he was judging each item as a whole as it would affect the normal person, and, in *Roth*, the trial judge instructed the jury as follows:

"The test is not whether it would arouse sexual desires or sexual impure thoughts in those comprising a particular segment of the community, the young, the immature, or the highly prudish, or would leave another segment, the scientific or highly educated or the so-called worldly wise and sophisticated indifferent and unmoved. . . .

"The test in each case is the effect of the book, picture, or publication considered as a whole, not upon any particular class, but upon all those whom it is likely to reach. In other words, you determine its impact upon the average person in the community. The books, pictures, and circulars must be judged as a whole, in their entire context, and you are not to consider detached or separate portions in reaching a conclusion. You judge the circulars, pictures and publications which have been put in evidence by present-day standards of the community. You may ask yourselves does it offend the common conscience of the community by present-day standards.

"In this case, ladies and gentlemen of the jury, you and you alone are the exclusive judges of what the common conscience of the community is, and, in determining that conscience, you are to consider the community as a whole, young and old, educated and uneducated, the religious and the irreligious - men, women and children."

It is argued that the statutes do not provide reasonably ascertainable standards of guilt and therefore [violate] the constitutional requirements of due process. . . .

[W]e hold that these statutes, applied according to the proper standard for judging obscenity, do not offend constitutional safeguards against convictions based upon protected material, or fail to give men in acting adequate notice of what is prohibited.

. . . . Alberts argues that, because his was a mail-order business, the California statute is repugnant to Article I, Section 8, clause 7, under which the Congress allegedly preempted the regulatory field by enacting the federal obscenity statute, punishing the mailing or advertising by mail of obscene material. The federal statute deals only with actual mailing; it does not eliminate the power of the state to punish "keeping for sale" or "advertising" obscene material. The state statute in no way imposes a burden or interferes with the federal postal functions. ". . . . The decided cases which indicate the limits of state regulatory power in relation to the federal mail service involve situations where state regulation involved a direct, physical interference with federal activities under the postal power or some direct, immediate burden on the performance of the postal functions. . . ."

The judgments are affirmed.

Appendix

[This case, which never reached the U.S. Supreme Court, is included for its significant impact on American obscenity and pornography law.]

The Trial of James Joyce's *Ulysses*

The importation into the United States from any foreign country of any book written with "pornographic intent," that is, written for the purpose of exploiting obscenity, is prohibited. A book will be deemed to be obscene if it tends to stir sex impulses or lead to sexually impure and lustful thoughts. **- The Obscenity Exclusion Act (1930)**

On February 2, 1922 Shakespeare & Company, a Paris bookstore, published the book that no one else would - James Joyce's *Ulysses*. Believed by many to be the greatest literary work of the twentieth century, *Ulysses* recounts, in strong language and intimate imagery, one day in the inner lives of Dublin's Leopold and Molly Bloom.

The United States Congress, under the Federal Obscenity Exclusion Act, made the importation into the United States of any "obscene or pornographic" books illegal. Officials of the United States Customs Service and the United States Post Office, holding that *Ulysses* was obscene under the law, seized imported copies and destroyed them by burning. Bootleg copies, purchased in Europe and smuggled into the United States, made the forbidden book a literary underground bestseller. In 1932, ten years after its original publication, Random House purchased for $1,500 the right to publish *Ulysses*. To bring a test case before an American court, Random House arranged to "smuggle" a copy of *Ulysses* into the United States. The copy was seized by the pre-warned Customs inspectors. The trial of James Joyce's *Ulysses* lasted two days.

On December 6, 1933 United States District Judge John Woolsey announced his decision. The unedited text of *U.S. v. Ulysses* can be found in volume 5 of the *Federal Supplement*. Our edited plain-English text follows.

THE TRIAL OF
JAMES JOYCE'S "ULYSSES"
December 6, 1933

JUDGE JOHN WOOLSEY: . . . . I have read [James Joyce's] *Ulysses* once in its entirety and I have read those passages of which the government particularly complains several times. In fact, for many weeks, my spare time has been devoted to the consideration of the decision which my duty would require me to make in this matter.

Ulysses is not an easy book to read or to understand. But there has been much written about it, and in order properly to approach the consideration of it, it is advisable to read a number of other books which have now become its satellites. The study of *Ulysses* is, therefore, a heavy task.

The reputation of *Ulysses* in the literary world, however, warranted my taking such time as was necessary to enable me to satisfy myself as to the intent with which the book was written, for, of course, in any case where a book is claimed to be obscene it must first be determined whether the intent with which it was written was what is called, according to the usual phrase, pornographic, that is, written for the purpose of exploiting obscenity.

If the conclusion is that the book is pornographic, that is the end of the inquiry and forfeiture must follow.

But in *Ulysses,* in spite of its unusual frankness, I do not detect anywhere the leer of the sensualist. I hold, therefore, this it is not pornographic.

In writing *Ulysses,* Joyce sought to make a serious experiment in a new, if not wholly novel, literary genre. He takes persons of the lower middle class living in Dublin in 1904 and seeks not only to describe what they did on a certain day early in June of that year as they went about the city bent on their usual occupations, but also to tell what many of them thought about the while.

Joyce has attempted - it seems to me, with astonishing success - to show how the screen of consciousness, with its ever-shifting kaleidoscopic impressions carries . . . not only what is in the focus of each man's observation of the actual things about him, but also . . . past impression[s]; some recent and some drawn up by association from the domain of the subconscious. He shows how each of these impressions affects the life and behavior of the character which he is describing.

What he seeks to get is not unlike the result of a double or . . . multiple exposure on a cinema film, which would give a clear foreground with a background visible but somewhat blurred and out of focus in varying degrees.

To convey by words an effect which obviously lends itself more appropriately to a graphic technique, accounts, it seems to me, for much of the obscurity which meets a reader of *Ulysses*. And it also explains another aspect of the book, which I have further to consider, namely, Joyce's sincerity and his honest effort to show exactly how the minds of his characters operate.

If Joyce did not attempt to be honest in developing the technique which he has adopted in *Ulysses*, the result would be psychologically misleading and thus unfaithful to his chosen technique. Such an attitude would be artistically inexcusable.

It is because Joyce has been loyal to his technique and has not funked its necessary implications - but has honestly attempted to tell fully what his characters think about - that he has been the subject of so many attacks and that his purpose has been so often misunderstood and misrepresented. For his attempt sincerely and honesty to realize his objective has required him incidentally to use certain words which are generally considered dirty words and has led at times to what many think is a too poignant preoccupation with sex in the thoughts of his characters.

The words which are criticized as dirty are old Saxon words known to almost all men and, I venture, to many women, and are such words as would be naturally and habitually used, I believe, by the types of folk whose life - physical and mental - Joyce is seeking to describe. In respect of the recurrent emergence of the theme of sex in the minds of his characters, it must always be remembered that his locale was Celtic and his season spring.

Whether or not one enjoys such a technique as Joyce uses is a matter of taste on which disagreement or argument is futile, but to subject that technique to the standards of some other technique seems to me to be little short of absurd.

Accordingly, I hold that *Ulysses* is a sincere and honest book and I think that the criticisms of it are entirely disposed of by its rationale.

Furthermore *Ulysses* is an amazing tour de force when one considers the success which has been in the main achieved with such a difficult objective as Joyce set for himself. As I have stated, *Ulysses* is not an easy book to read. It is brilliant and dull, intelligible and obscure, by turns. In many places it seems to me to be disgusting, but although it contains, as I have mentioned above, many words usually considered dirty, I have not found anything that I consider to be dirt for dirt's sake. Each word of the book contributes like a bit of mosaic to the detail of the picture which Joyce is seeking to construct for his readers.

If one does not wish to associate with such folk as Joyce describes, that is one's own choice. In order to avoid indirect contact with them one may not wish to read *Ulysses;* that is quite understandable. But when such a great artist in words, as Joyce undoubtedly is, seeks to draw a true picture of the lower middle class in a European city, ought it to be impossible for the American public legally to see that picture?

To answer this question it is not sufficient merely to find, as I have found above, that Joyce did not write *Ulysses* with what is commonly called pornographic intent; I must endeavor to apply a more objective standard to his book in order to determine its effect in the result, irrespective of the intent with which it was written.

The statute under which the libel is filed only denounces, in so far as we are here concerned, the importation into the United States from any foreign country of "any obscene book." It does not marshal against books the spectrum of condemnatory adjectives found, commonly, in laws dealing with matters of this kind. I am, therefore, only required to determine whether *Ulysses* is obscene within the legal definition of that word.

The meaning of the word "obscene" as legally defined by the courts is - Tending to stir the sex impulses or to lead to sexually impure and lustful thoughts.

Whether a particular book would tend to excite such impulses and thoughts must be tested by the court's opinion as to its effect on a person with average sex instincts - what the French would call *l'homme moyen sensuel* - who plays, in this branch of legal inquiry, the same role of hypothetical reagent as does the "reasonable man" in the law of torts and "the man learned in the art" on questions of invention in patent law.

. . . . After I had made my decision in regard to the aspect of *Ulysses* now under consideration, I checked my impressions with two friends of mine who in my opinion [would be objective].

These literary assessors - as I might properly describe them - were called on separately, and neither knew that I was consulting the other. They are men whose opinion on literature and on life I value most highly. They had both read *Ulysses*, and, of course, were wholly unconnected with this cause.

Without letting either of my assessors know what my decision was, I gave to each of them the legal definition of obscene and asked each whether in his opinion *Ulysses* was obscene within that definition.

I was interested to find that they both agreed with my opinion - that reading *Ulysses* in its entirety, as a book must be read on such a test as this, did not tend to excite sexual impulses or lustful thoughts, but that its net effect on them was only that of a somewhat tragic and very powerful commentary on the inner lives of men and women.

It is only with the normal person that the law is concerned. Such a test as I have described, therefore, is the only proper test of obscenity in the case of a book like *Ulysses*, which is a sincere and serious attempt to devise a new literary method for the observation and description of mankind.

I am quite aware that owing to some of its scenes *Ulysses* is a rather strong draught to ask some sensitive, though normal, persons to take. But my considered opinion, after long reflection, is that, whilst in many places the effect of *Ulysses* on the reader undoubtedly is somewhat emetic, nowhere does it tend to be an aphrodisiac.

Ulysses may, therefore, be admitted into the United States.

Bibliography

Anastopio, George. *Freedom of Speech and the First Amendment.* Detroit, MI: University of Detroit Law Journal, 1964.

Anonymous. *Go Ask Alice.* New York, NY: Avon Books, 1982.

Baker, C. Edwin. *Human Liberty and Freedom of Speech.* New York, NY: Oxford University Press, 1989.

Barron, Jerome A., and C. Thomas Dienes. *Handbook of Free Speech and Free Press.* Boston, MA: Little, Brown, 1979.

Bosmajian, Haig A. *Freedom of Expression.* New York, NY: Neal-Schuman, 1988.

_____. *The Freedom to Read.* New York, NY: Neal-Schuman, 1987.

Burress, Lee. *Battle of the Books: Literary Censorship in the Public Schools, 1950-1985.* Metuchen, NJ: Scarecrow Press, 1989.

Caristi, Dom. *Expanding Free Expression in the Marketplace: Broadcasting and the Public Forum.* New York, NY: Quorum Books, 1992.

Carter, T. Barton, Marc A. Franklin, and Jay B. Wright. *The First Amendment and the Fifth Estate: Regulation of Electronic Mass Media.* Mineola, NY: Foundation Press, 1986.

Chaffee, Zachariah. *Free Speech in the United States.* Cambridge, MA: Harvard University Press, 1967.

Childress, Alice. *A Hero Ain't Nothin' But a Sandwich.* New York, NY: Coward McCann, 1973.

Cleaver, Eldridge. *Soul on Ice.* New York, NY: McGraw-Hill, 1968.

Cox, Archibald. *The Court and the Constitution.* New York, NY: Houghton-Mifflin, 1988.

Easton, Susan M. *The Problem of Pornography: Regulation and the Right to Free Speech.* New York, NY: Routledge, 1994.

Friedman, Leon, comp. *Obscenity: The Complete Oral Arguments Before the Supreme Court in the Major Obscenity Cases.* New York, NY: Chelsea House Publishers, 1970.

Gerber, Albert B. *Sex, Pornography, and Justice.* New York, NY: L. Stuart, 1965.

Greenawalt, Kent. *Fighting Words: Individuals, Communities and Liberties of Speech.* Princeton, NJ: Princeton University, 1995.

Gurstein, Rochelle. *The Repeal of Reticence: A History of America's Cultural and Legal Struggles Over Free Speech, Obscenity, Sexual Liberation, and Modern Art.* New York, NY: Hill & Wang, 1996.

Hemmer, Joseph J. *The Supreme Court and the First Amendment.* New York, NY: Random House, 1991.

Hentoff, Nat. *The First Freedom: A Tumultuous History of Free Speech in America.* New York, NY: Delacorte Press, 1980.

Hixson, Richard F. *Pornography and the Justices: The Supreme Court and the Intractable Obscenity Problem.* Carbondale, IL: Southern Illinois University Press, 1996.

Hughes, Langston, Editor. *The Best Short Stories of Negro Writers.* Boston, MA: Little, Brown, 1967.

Kalven, Harry, Jr. *A Worthy Tradition: Freedom of Speech in America.* New York, NY: Harper & Row, 1988.

LaFarge, Oliver. *Laughing Boy.* New York, NY: Houghton-Mifflin, 1929.

Leahy, James E. *The First Amendment, 1791-1991: Two Hundred Years of Freedom.* Jefferson, NC: McFarland & Co., 1991.

Leone, Bruno, Editor. *Free Speech.* San Diego, CA: Greenhaven Press, 1994.

Morris, Desmond. *The Naked Ape.* New York, NY: McGraw-Hill, 1967.

Noble, William. *Bookbanning in America: Who Bans Books? And Why?* Middlebury, VT: P.S. Eriksson, 1990.

Paul, James C.N., and Murray L. Schwartz. *Federal Censorship: Obscenity in the Mail.* New York, NY: Free Press of Glencoe, 1961.

Rembar, Charles. *The End of Obscenity: The Trials of Lady Chatterley, Tropic of Cancer, and Fanny Hill.* New York, NY: Harper & Row, 1986.

Schwartz, Bernard. *Freedom of the Press.* New York, NY: Facts on File, 1992.

Shaughnessy, Edward J., and Diana Trebbi. *A Standard for Miller: A Community Response to Pornography.* Lanham, MD: University Press of America, 1980.

Spitzer, Matthew L. *Seven Dirty Words and Six Other Stories: Controlling the Content of Print and Broadcast.* New Haven, CT: Yale University Press, 1986.

Stevens, John D. *Shaping the First Amendment: The Development of Free Expression.* Beverly Hills, CA: Sage Publications, 1982.

Sunstein, Cass R. *Democracy and the Problems of Free Speech.* New York, NY: The Free Press, 1993.

Thomas, Piri. *Down These Mean Streets.* New York, NY: Knopf, 1967.

Vonnegut, Kurt. *Slaughterhouse Five.* New York, NY: Delacorte Press, 1994.

Wagman, Robert J. *The First Amendment Book.* New York, NY: World Almanac, 1991.

Worton, Stanley N. *Freedom of Speech and Press.* Rochelle Park, NJ: Hayden Book Co., 1975.

Wright, Richard. *Black Boy.* New York, NY: Caedmon, 1989.

Index

EXCELLENT BOOKS ORDER FORM

(Please xerox this form so it will be available to other readers.)

Please send
Copy(ies)

_____ of OBSCENITY & PORNOGRAPHY DECISIONS @ $16.95
_____ of LANDMARK DECISIONS I @ $16.95
_____ of LANDMARK DECISIONS II @ $16.95
_____ of LANDMARK DECISIONS III @ $16.95
_____ of LANDMARK DECISIONS IV @ $16.95
_____ of LANDMARK DECISIONS V @ $16.95
_____ of LANDMARK DECISIONS VI @ $16.95
_____ of SCHOOLHOUSE DECISIONS @ $16.95
_____ of LIFE, DEATH, AND THE LAW @ $16.95
_____ of FREEDOM OF SPEECH DECISIONS @ $16.95
_____ of FREEDOM OF THE PRESS DECISIONS @ $16.95
_____ of FREEDOM OF RELIGION DECISIONS @ $16.95
_____ of THE MURDER REFERENCE @ $16.95
_____ of THE RAPE REFERENCE @ $16.95
_____ of ABORTION DECISIONS: THE 1970's @ $16.95
_____ of ABORTION DECISIONS: THE 1980's @ $16.95
_____ of ABORTION DECISIONS: THE 1990's @ $16.95
_____ of CIVIL RIGHTS DECISIONS: 19th CENTURY @ $16.95
_____ of CIVIL RIGHTS DECISIONS: 20th CENTURY @ $16.95
_____ of THE ADA HANDBOOK @ $16.95

Name: _____

Address: _____

City: _____ State: _____ Zip: _____

Add $1 per book for shipping and handling.
California residents add sales tax.

OUR GUARANTEE: Any Excellent Book may be returned at
any time for any reason and a full refund will be made.

Mail your check or money order to: Excellent Books,
Post Office Box 131322, Carlsbad, California 92013-1322
Call: 760-598-5069/Fax: 240-218-7601/E-mail: xlntbks@aol.com